LABOR
UP-FRONT

Report to the 22nd Convention
of the Communist Party, U.S.A.
Detroit, Mich., August 23, 1979

International Publishers, New York

LABOR UP-FRONT

In the People's Fight Against the Crisis

by Gus Hall

Library of Congress Cataloging in Publication Data

Hall, Gus
    Labor up-front in the people's fight against the crisis.

    1.   Communist Party of the United States of America.
22d convention, Detroit, 1979.   2.   Communism—United
States—1917-   —Congresses.   I.   Communist Party of
the United States of America.   22d convention, Detroit,
1979.   II.   Title.
JK2391.C5A35   329'.82'0221   79-26569
ISBN 0-7178-0565-4

Contents

LABOR
UP-FRONT

History's Bouquet

For those who fight on the progressive side of human affairs the struggles present their own awards and honors. And at critical turning points history presents its bouquets of approval.

Holding our National Convention here in Michigan, at the municipally-owned Cobo Hall is such an award, such an honor. It is history's bouquet of approval. It is also history's way of tweaking the nose of the corporate structure.

Sixty years ago the corporate establishment saw a specter. U.S. capitalism mobilized for all-out war against it. They pulled out all stops to prevent the birth of a working class revolutionary party that advocated socialism.

They mobilized the police force and the courts. They trained a stable of provocateurs and stoolpigeons. They launched the most intensive and vile campaign of slander and falsehoods. They passed laws making Marxist thought illegal. They sent hundreds to prison, conducted mass raids, deported thousands and created a caste system of unemployables. They promoted and pushed racism on a mass scale. And yes, they murdered and maimed.

In spite of all their efforts, 60 years ago a group of heroic men and women—the best thinkers, the most advanced revolutionary minds—gathered in Bridgman, Michigan to attend a convention of the newly born Communist Party. This was a bold move. It was a small gathering. But the capitalist class saw it as the handwriting on the wall. They attacked with full force—federal, state and city—the FBI, the police. The Mayor of Bridgman joined the vigilantes. They arrested the leaders and confiscated the draft resolutions. They celebrated, believing that the specter was buried in the sand dunes near Bridgman, Michigan.

After 60 short years, after McCarthy, the Smith Act, Communist Control Act, after Leavenworth, Atlanta and Terre Haute—here we are—at Cobo Hall. We are here because the Communist Party, USA is on the progressive side of human affairs, on the working class side of the class struggle.

Our being here, at Cobo Hall, is in a sense an award, an honor bestowed on our Party by the class struggle.

Our being here is a bouquet of approval and a vote of confidence by history.

60th Anniversary

This is a special—a most glorious occasion. In addition to holding our 22nd National Convention, we are celebrating 60 meaningful, exciting years of the Communist Party, USA.

We were formed as a Communist Party in September 1919. That is an historic date.

Our Party came into existence, at a turning point in world affairs and in the international working class movement, created by the development of imperialism, the catastrophic First World War, and the outbreak of the great Russian Revolution that gave birth to the first workers' government, the Soviet Union. These history-making events affected every part of the world, including the United States. These events had their influence on, and contributed to the founding of the Communist Party, USA.

Contrary to the red-baiting slander, our Party was not formed from "the outside." It was created by the conditions and the social forces within our own country. It was a response to the sufferings, caused by the war, of the masses of our people. It was a response to the corporate juggernaut of exploitation, to the racism, the high prices and lowered living standards—while the bankers and industrialists made fabulous profits.

The war and the economic conditions led to big strikes, mass discontent and growing radicalism. Capitalism was leading the United States into a dead-end alley.

Our origins really date far back to the first Marxist groups formed in the 1850s. The early Marxists helped nominate Abraham Lincoln as a candidate for the presidency, fought in the Civil War, prodded Lincoln to a bolder strategy in organizing Afro-Americans of the North and removing the racist obstacles to their full participation in the Civil War; they also helped to work out a strategy which hastened the victory and crushed the rebellion of the slaveholders.

The work of the Communist Party since its formation, despite severe repression and periods of illegality, has been considerable. There is not a single important issue or struggle since 1919 that the Communist Party has failed to take part in or to lead.

Our Party helped to bring about unemployment insurance through tremendous mass struggles. We were in the forefront in the fight for social security. Communists contributed to the movement and tactics of the CIO for the organization of the unorganized in the basic mass production industries.

We have fought in the civil rights battles against the racist oppression of Black Americans, Chicanos and other oppressed nationalities.

We fought to save Republican Spain from Franco fascism. The majority of the 1,500 U.S. volunteers who died on that battlefield were members of our Party.

We fought against the fascist threat to our country by the Nazis, who were aided by the most reactionary sections of U.S. monopoly capital. And we fought side-by-side with our countrymen in the war against Hitler fascism and Japanese imperialism.

We made contributions in the struggles for the independence of Cuba and Angola, China and the Philippines, Nicaragua and Puerto Rico, and all who fight to break the stranglehold of U.S. imperialism.

We participated in the struggles against U.S. aggression in Korea and Vietnam, and generally in the intense struggles of our people to defeat McCarthyism and defend the democratic rights of all Americans.

In all of these, and other significant daily struggles of our people, our Party has been and is a diligent, heroic, earnest and intelligent forefront fighter. We can truly be proud of our Party's history.

If our advance was checked in the latter 1950s and 1960s it was because of the extreme repression of McCarthyism. It was the worst campaign of terror and repression against labor and all progressive forces in our history—the effects of which we have gradually overcome, despite continuing anti-communism.

On our 60th birthday the Communist Party, USA remains a viable, growing and active force in our country, one that has been molded and tempered through 60 years of U.S. history.

Moreover, we are proud of the fact that our Party is part of the world Communist movement, which now exists in over 100 countries and has more than 70 million members.

Marxism and the Communists are the greatest political force in the world because they are on the right side of history.

We are part of the world revolutionary process that is sweeping aside imperialist oppression.

We are part of the inevitable historic tide of world socialism.

Two Classes—Two Political Parties

The people of Michigan have an unusual opportunity to compare two political conventions of two political parties representing the interests and viewpoints of the two opposite ends of the economic and political spectrum—two parties representing two classes.

As you know, the Republican Party will follow the Communist Party to Cobo Hall. And as we also know, the Republican Party, as well as the Democratic Party, represent and work for the basic interests of the large stockholders of General Motors, the Fords and Chrysler. This is their sole purpose in life.

We of the Communist Party represent and work for the best interests of the workers of General Motors, Ford and Chrysler.

The Republican Party convention will say nothing about the closing of the Dodge Main plant, or the 6,000 families whose economic lifeline is being coldbloodedly cut—thrown on the scrap heap as if they were used-up spark plugs. We say the closing of Dodge Main is an irresponsible—a criminal—act.

The Republicans will say—the Chrysler Corporation has a right to close the plant, and that the union, the workers and the government have no right to interfere with this act of a free enterprise.

What irony—at the same time it is closing the Dodge Main plant, Chrysler is asking for a billion dollar handout of people's tax dollars.

We say the closing of the plant infringes on the most basic of all human rights—the right to make a living.

The Republicans will say the corporations have a right to make a profit, and therefore the right to close this plant because it does not produce *maximum* profits. We say private corporate profits are not a right, any more than is highway robbery.

We say there is only one fundamental right, and one responsibility. That is for the workers and their families to be able to live— to feed and clothe their families, and to be able to send their children to school. There is nothing in life that can supersede that right.

So we say to Chrysler and to the Republican Party—we will do all we can to make it possible for the workers at the Dodge plant, and people of Detroit, to say: "This is our plant. This is our city. This is where we have to make our living. We're not going to let some thieving corporate executives arbitrarily cut our lifeline. Either you run the plant, or we will."

The Republican and Democratic parties are parties of Big Business. We are the party of the people, the working class. That is why we are on opposite sides of most issues.

The Republican and Democratic parties are parties of an economic system and a class that is on its way out—because it is a system and a class of exploitation and racism, a class that accepts no social responsibility.

The Communist Party is a party of the class that is on its way up. We are for a socio-economic system that will put an end to exploitation of the workers—forever; put an end to private profits—forever; an end to racism—forever; an end to plant closings, job insecurity and unemployment—forever; an end to war and war production—forever. That is why we are for socialism.

2

The Economic—Political Situation

Our 22nd National Convention is taking place at a tremendously important moment. Even if our Party's Constitution did not require that we call a national convention at this time, the political and economic developments would have made it necessary.

This is one of those moments when a number of developments and movements are building up a head of steam. What adds a special, critical quality to these developments is the fact that they are taking place simultaneously—converging like whirlwinds moving in the same direction, creating a political force that can grow to hurricane proportions.

When the president takes to the hills to hide, the storm warnings must be taken seriously indeed by all of us.

The State of State Monopoly Capitalism

The economy is in an economic recession that can—and most likely will—develop into a full-blown economic crisis. It will be severe and could be of long duration.

The new round of layoffs and plant closings have begun. Inflation is completely out of control. Prices, rents and taxes continue on a monthly upward spiral. When measured by the yardstick of food, clothing, housing, transportation and medical care, the inflation rate is now 18.5 percent.

This is indeed the age of ripoffs. The people are being ripped off on all sides—at every turn. The shortages and runaway prices of gasoline and heating oil are adding a new dimension to the crisis of everyday living. For many in the northern cities this winter will be a new "ice age." There is even talk about building refugee camps for the victims of heatless homes.

Government bodies are in a state of paralysis. The two parties of Big Business are in disarray. The dollar continues to flounder on the world money exchanges. The United States trade balance continues heavily on the deficit side.

The economy suffers from a mixture of short-range cyclical and long-range chronic problems. And there is a continuing deterioration in the overall structural framework of United States capitalism. There is instability and a depletion of reserves. The quality of life continues to decline.

The temper of the people has shifted from disappointment to frustration to anger. There is a new spontaneous explosiveness among the masses that keeps surfacing, even in unexpected sectors, such as the independent truckers and farmers.

There is much confusion and the developments are uneven. But the overwhelming sentiment of the people is anti-corporate and anti-state. They rate the president and the presidency at an all-time low.

This is but a reflection of the fact that the public is giving the lowest possible ratings to corporations, to Congress, to federal, state and local governing bodies. Further, they are increasingly giving a low rating to the whole capitalist system.

In a recent Hart Poll, by a majority of 58 to 25 percent, the people voted that they believe: "The major corporations tend to dominate and determine the actions of the public figures in Washington." By a majority of 57 to 35 percent, they voted that: "Both the Democratic and Republican Parties are in favor of Big Business." And by a vote of 66 to 20 percent they "favored employee ownership and control of the large corporations." Fifty six percent said they would "vote for candidates who favored employee ownership."

President Carter is right; there is a sense of malaise in some quarters. Some time ago the *Harvard Business Review* asked its high level corporate readers: "Which of the two ideologies—capitalism or socialism—will prevail in the United States by the mid-1980s?" Seventy three percent said they believed capitalism will be largely replaced by some kind of socialist order.

Excluding the corporate executives, of course, there is a shift in a radical direction. It is a growing mood that reflects a declining confidence in the system. There is a growing mood for more than the usual run-of-the-mill reforms. It is a shift toward support for more basic radical structural changes. The mood is now overwhelmingly and solidly anti-corporate, anti-monopoly and anti-state.

We are again living at one of those major crossroads. State monopoly capitalism has developed to a level where the usual reform measures have little effect and the anti-monopoly movements have not yet reached a level where they can compel more radical measures.

To this point, the responses of state monopoly capitalism—in spite of the crises—are measures that are at the expense of the people, and policies that continue to feed and fatten the corporate golden calf.

Carter, *The New York Times* and the whole monopoly complex keep asking for "a high level of public sacrifice," while the corporations are making windfall profits at every turn of events.

We are in a period when masses have lost confidence in the old ruling structure, including the two old parties, but have not yet placed their trust in new political formations. We are at a moment when the majority are dissatisfied and are not willing to go along with the way things are, but not yet clear how things should be.

We are in a phase where the masses are angry and ready for action, but are not yet quite clear as to how and where to direct their anger.

As usual, this crossroad presents both a great potential for progress. But it also contains the potential danger of setbacks, the danger of misuse and manipulation of the anger and militancy by reactionary Right-wing forces.

It is also one of those moments when because of our Party's social science, because of our understanding of the class struggle, our understanding of the laws of capitalist development, of the role of the masses and movements, we can make the difference. We can be the key factor in deciding what direction our country will take from this crossroad; how and at whose expense the crisis will be solved.

Cut Throat Exploitation

The main cause—the root of all the crises—is embedded in the economic structure, in the inherent laws of capitalist development.

If a warning signal was needed about the new level of brutal, cut-throat exploitation of our working class, the surpassing of the 100 billion dollar mark, in clear take-home profits by the corporations, should have set off the alarm. These annual, after-taxes profits are now reaching the 150 billion dollar mark.

Corporate profits have more than tripled in the last 10 years. This has taken place during a period when production has been almost stagnant, and at a moment when United States capitalism is suffering some serious setbacks in many areas of the world.

These record-making profits cannot be explained by inflation. They are the result of the speedup and sweat, blood and toil of the workers, and of cuts in real wages. The huge corporate profits are directly related to the decline in both relative and real wages. The continuing, absolute decline in real wages is a new phenomenon in our times. The high rate of exploitation of our working class and the resulting surplus value continue to increase at a fast clip. And the high rate of inflation adds but another element to this system of exploitation.

This unprecedented high rate of surplus value is made possible because of the monopoly domination of the entire production and distribution cycle. It is the end product of the operation of the law of maximum profits under conditions of state monopoly capitalism. The fundamental capitalist law of surplus value and the drive for maximum profits have not changed. But the rapid development of state monopoly capitalism and the expanding role of the state have changed the conditions under which these laws operate.

The tripling of corporate profits in a ten year period is a direct result of these changed conditions. It is a direct corporate expropriation from the intensified exploitation of the working class—through speedup, overtime, and the neglect and violation of health and safety requirements. It is possible because of the super-exploitation of racially and nationally oppressed peoples—Afro-Americans, Puerto Ricans and Chicanos—some 40 million people altogether. It is the end product of monopoly control of the scientific and technological revolution, which enables the monopolies in the most advanced branches of industry to set prices that are many times the cost of production. It is also possible because of the superprofits from the export of capital (foreign investment) which increases at a faster rate than domestic investment, to areas where the payment of wages is often a fraction of that in the United States.

The tripling of profits is possible because of the role of the state. With the rise of corporate profits there is a related rise in strike-breaking court injunctions and strike-related police brutality.

There are government subsidies to monopolies in various forms: turning over the fruits of government-financed research and development to private corporations; the systematic shifting of the tax burden to reduce the portion taken out of corporate profits and increase the portion taken out of wages; the use of state power to enforce "income policies" which put limits on wages and insures the increase in the rate of surplus value; the use of military and financial power to force open new spheres of foreign investment for monopoly capital; the awarding of government contracts, especially military contracts, on terms assuring fabulous superprofits; there is the rapid turnover of the national debt at rising interest rates, services on which now amount to over 50 billion dollars annually.

These are just some of the areas where the state has a direct hand in providing the basis for the higher rate of exploitation and surplus value.

In spite of all the claims to the contrary, the huge corporate profits come from an increasing rate of productivity, which again means an increasing rate of exploitation of the working class. Because monopoly capital has slowed down the rate of capital investment on new machinery the rate of productivity increasingly comes from speeding up the processes of production.

Corporate profits soaring as never before. Real wages declining as never before. This is the economic bottom line. This is the objective setting for the class struggle for this period of time.

Because of the high degree of state monopoly control, the economic crisis takes on some new contradictory aspects. There is the high and rising rate of unemployment, and the rising rate of inflation. Plants are being mothballed, while corporate profits keep breaking records. Housing construction is on the decline, but interest rates keep going up. The taxes the rich and the corporations pay are being cut, but the taxes the workers pay are being increased. There is an economic crisis, but no crisis in the stock market reflecting the high monopoly prices.

There is much talk about affirmative action to undo the wrongs of the past. But the new layoffs and plant closings are continuing the same racist patterns of last-to-be-hired, first-to-be-fired. As the crisis and unemployment increase, women and young workers are being sent back into the reserve labor pool.

The guns-or-butter dilemma has reached a new crisis point. The military budgets have become a heavy counterweight to all economic processes. They add to inflation and unemployment. They add depth and length to the economic crisis.

3

The Energy Crisis

The problems arising from the energy crisis are adding a new dimension to the other crisis areas. They are adding a new quality to all contradictions. They are affecting the patterns of economic cycles.

The crisis of energy has elevated the level of anger and frustration of the people to a boiling point. Most people instinctively place the blame where it belongs—on the oil monopolies.

Because they know who the real culprit is, people get even more outraged and disgusted when they read about a top Carter aide

advising the President to *"make* OPEC the enemy," and telling
Carter, "You must have the *appearance* in the next weeks of doing
something about the energy crisis." Or when Schlesinger testified
that we dare not make the oil corporations comply with the laws of
the land or the needs of the people because "they may *retaliate."*
"They may keep the oil on the high seas." That's the voice of a
servant of the oil monopolies.

It is undeniable: there is concealment; there is subterfuge and
there are conspiracies. But there is no big mystery about the crisis of
energy. There is a coverup of the same three key words—maximum
corporate profits.

The long lines at the gas pumps are a creation of the oil monopolies and Carter's Department of Energy. They are the inevitable
result of a ten-year policy of not increasing refining capacity to
meet rising needs.

This policy is geared to keeping supply very close to the level of
demand. This makes it easier to manipulate and create crises.
Starting some five months ago, the corporations, with the Energy
Department's sanction, decided to cut the supply below demand
by simply cutting refining to below 85 percent of capacity. The
predictable result is shortages at the gas pump, which are now used
by the oil monopolies to justify the escalating prices and to get the
government to lift all price regulations and controls.

It set the stage for Carter to announce in April that starting June 1
the oil corporations could begin the process of raising the price of
domestic oil to the level of imported oil. This was the same as
saying: "Don't sell your gas now. Hold on, and after June 1 you can
add a windfall profit."

There is such irony in these developments. One day Carter
attacks the OPEC countries, charging them with irresponsibly
ripping off the consumers. The next day he issues an executive
order giving the U.S. oil corporations the go-ahead to match the
OPEC prices on domestic oil. Carter says the OPEC prices are a
ripoff, but the same price charged for oil from domestic production
is a "needed incentive."

There is also a coverup of the fact that much of the OPEC oil
comes from wells still partly owned and largely refined and distributed by the same U.S. oil monopolies.

So the shortages at the gas pumps were created by the manipula-
tions of the oil monopolies, with the aid of the government.

The shortages are also used to bamboozle the public into believing that if the monopolies could make more profits they would spend it on increased exploration for oil and gas. If higher profits resulted in more exploration for oil, by now we would be swimming in oil.

The U.S. oil monopolies plead poverty—with assets of 155 billion dollars, with accumulated earnings of over 60 billion dollars, and with this year's profits running at the rate of 20 billion dollars. And the $20 billion does not include the $10 or $15 billion they will get after the windfall profits tax that Congress and the Carter Administration are handing to them.

There is much talk about gasoline shortages. But when the gas lines in California and New York were the longest these same oil pirates were peddling gas, refined in U.S. plants, on the world market to the highest bidder. And, as was to be expected, now that the price controls have been removed and the gas is over $1 per gallon, the refineries are operating at 90 percent of capacity and the lines at the gas pumps have disappeared.

In comparison to the Rockefeller-Schlesinger ripoff, the Brink's robberies are like dips into the petty-cash funds.

By and large the Carter Administration and the mass media have adopted the "make OPEC the enemy" line. It is so convenient to point the finger at a "foreign enemy," while ripping off the people.

Here is how the total dollar we pay at the gas pumps is divided— for foreign and domestic oil: the oil monopolies take 40¢; the U.S. government takes 25¢, and the OPEC governments get 13¢. The rest is divided among smaller oil pipeline hangers-on.

The "make OPEC the enemy" campaign is more than finding a scapegoat. It is in line with the preparations for military takeover of the "enemy."

Not because of foresight, but because it has been able to get oil at a cheap colonial price, U.S. imperialism has used more and more imported oil, while saving the domestic sources. The United States has been the most greedy looter of all the imperialist oil-suckers. But this colonial exploitation of the oil reserves of the developing countries could not continue forever.

So capitalism now faces the effects of being cut off from cheap oil. And capitalism was caught unprepared for these changes in the field of energy. A year ago they were still talking about "breaking the OPEC cartel."

That is one side—the immediate side—of the energy crisis. The shortages at the gas pumps are not directly related to a more basic world energy crisis that is now appearing on the horizon.

For the world, the shadows of depletion—of easy-to-get-at cheap sources of energy—are beginning to appear at the end of the tunnel of energy.

For over 100 years oil and gas have served as a main source of energy. It is now calculated that the easy-to-get-at sources of oil and gas will enter the age of depletion in our lifetime. And uranium, which feeds the nuclear plants, is joining the parade of early depletion. These three sources are non-renewable and now definitely limited.

At present, there are no other alternate, easy-to-get-at or cheap renewable sources of energy available. For this reason, each day the world is moving closer to a qualitatively different energy/life relationship. This is a new problem. Increasingly this will become a new factor affecting all economic, political and social developments.

It greatly adds to all contradictions and relationships. It adds a new wrinkle to the class struggle. It adds a new dimension to the anti-imperialist struggle. It adds a new ingredient to the transition to socialism.

The energy crisis brings out the basic thieving, predatory inner-nature of imperialism. There is a growing open advocacy of U.S. military intervention, for military takeover of the oil fields. Such corporate voices as *The New York Times* and *Wall Street Journal* are warning about the inadvisability of such actions now. But editorially, they are both keeping the options open. For example, *The New York Times* foresees that "there may be reason someday for the United States to seize a foreign oil field," and Senator Gary Hart echoes these sentiments: "We may be forced to use military forces to preserve the oil flow." And these are the voices of moderation.

And of course there is more than just talk. There is the continuing buildup of a "U.S. military presence" in the Mideast and the Persian Gulf and Indian Ocean. The Pentagon is in the process of training an intervention task force, specifically trained for action around oil fields. This force is being trained for "desert warfare." The depletion of resources increases the danger of war.

This developing oil crisis is also an additional pressure on the already existing tendencies toward polycentrism in the capitalist sector of the world. Each of the major capitalist countries is working to corner as much as possible of the world's fuel resources.

Up to this point in history, revolutionary changes in socio-economic systems have been propelled by changes and advances in technology and the development of ever-cheaper and easier-to-get-at energy sources. Slavery, feudalism and capitalism were all responses to ever-cheaper and available sources of energy. Human societies have never had to face the problem of the depletion of the main source of easy-to-get-at energy before new sources were available.

This presents a particular and difficult challenge to capitalism. The age of depletion forces a consideration of a basic restructuring of the energy complex. Because of long-range planning the Soviet Union and other socialist countries are well into the process of restructuring their energy complex. These changes are relatively easier for the socialist countries because they operate under one guiding principle: what is best for society as a whole is also best for each individual, and visa versa.

The management of shortages and the transition to alternative sources of energy are going to take a lot of concentrated effort; huge amounts of resources and careful long-range planning will be necessary. It has to be a top priority for a large section of the scientific community. And these changes will not pay off in dividends for a long time. The long-range interests of society as a whole will have to get top billing.

These pre-conditions all go against the very inner grain of capitalism. The anarchistic nature of capitalism and the singleminded corporate drive for private profits are a difficult, if not insurmountable, obstacle in the path of achieving the transition to new sources of energy. It is difficult, if not impossible, for private capital to manage the transition from the irrational, wasteful consumption of energy—which has reached its extreme in the United States—to a planned, unselfish consumption that corresponds to available supply. And this must be done without plunder or ripoff—both of which are inherent in capitalism.

The cannonized and idealized concepts ingrained in the capitalist production process—such as, "charge whatever the market will bear," or "above all else drive for maximum profits," or "what's good for GM is good for the country,"—are on a collision course with the problems involved in the energy crisis. The energy crisis adds another element to the general crisis of capitalism.

The energy crisis also brings into new focus some old crimes of capitalism—for example, the General Motors-Standard Oil conspiracy that has not only held back mass transit but has, rail by rail, destroyed much of the best energy-saving transit systems in many of the urban centers, as well as the railroad passenger system.

The energy crisis will force a restructuring of priorities. For monopoly capitalism this is a most difficult undertaking.

At the present time, the Carter Administration refuses to spend $70 to improve subway tunnels in the cities, but goes ahead with plans for spending $70 billion to build hundreds of miles of tunnels for the MX missiles.

There are other sources of energy—such as coal, tar sand, shale and solar. And of course, the source of all sources—the process of fusion.

Fusion has the potential of being an inexhaustible source. The Carter Administration and Congress are ready to earmark 100 billion dollars for the development of some of these sources. But there is a basic flaw in these plans, which will remain an obstacle to the necessary restructuring of the energy complex. And this is, that the new money will be given to the same old monopolies that have created the mess in the first place. It will be another ripoff.

The problems around nuclear power are in the very center of the restructuring of the energy complex. If the Three Mile Island nuclear disaster teaches anything, it is that private corporations should never have been permitted anywhere near the nuclear plants. They cannot be trusted with anything that presents such a potential danger to health and safety. Three Mile Island is also proof that the government agencies—as they are now constituted— cannot be trusted with the health and safety of the people.

Therefore, the question of the peaceful uses of nuclear power under capitalism should go back to square one. It means:

1) Remove the private corporations from the nuclear power field;

2) Close all existing plants. Ground them like the DC-10s were, because it is now clear there are some defective components and serious flaws in the design in all of them;

3) Set up people's committees, which would include trade unionists, scientists and consumers. Such committees should have the power to determine all questions of safety, including the very difficult question of the proper disposal of radioactive wastes.

There are a number of necessary and practical steps that can be taken in the field of energy that would guarantee that it is not the people who will pay for the shortages or the transition to new sources.

Only under public-government management can the use of the remaining old resources and the development of and transition to new sources be planned and orderly. Therefore, private corporations and private profits should be completely eliminated from the field of energy and

1) The energy complex should be nationalized—owned and operated under a democratically constituted public management;

2) The Pentagon is the biggest single user and waster of fuel. Therefore, cut the military allocations in half and release the three-year supply now being hoarded by the Pentagon;

3) Close all the nuclear plants run by the Pentagon, which are now operating without any kind of regulations or controls;

4) Distribute $1,000 worth of fuel stamps per year to all those on social security, welfare and to families whose income is less than $20,000 per year;

5) Set aside 10 billion dollars per year for the building of new mass transit systems. A few years ago there were 62,000 railroad passenger cars, now there are 12,000. In the last 5 years only 33 cars have been added;

6) Spend whatever is necessary for research and development of coal, solar and wind energy—but keep the greedy hands of the private corporations out of the process.

These and similar measures are necessary in the process of restructuring the energy complex.

The energy crisis makes the transition to socialism even more of a historic necessity. The depletion of some of the non-renewable sources of energy raises more urgently the need to scrap a socio-economic system that is also non-renewable and is rapidly being depleted of its internal energy. The crisis of energy argues for socialism. The solutions require placing people's interests above corporate interests.

The problems of the energy crisis and the developing economic crisis have become interlinked. Together they are giving rise to new problems. In the very center of these crises is the old basic question: at whose expense will the solutions be? So far, only the people are being ripped off.

4

United States—World Relations

The basic direction of world events is clear and unmistakable, while the specifics are often complex, contradictory and uneven.

The main opposing political and social forces are also clearly recognizable. But within each camp there are divisions, hesitations, confusion and wavering. Therefore, at moments of explosive historic change it is very important to keep one's eye on the overall direction of developments, on the main forces, and not become confused and entangled in secondary complexities.

With this in mind, the Draft Main Political Resolution (Draft MPR) very correctly places the question of the direction and the main forces contending on the world scene.

Let me quote from the Draft Main Political Resolution:

> The world revolutionary process has emerged as the irreversible line of development. It is the trunkline and the mainstay of all social progress. It is the only avenue open for the advancement of civilization. The forces that propel the world revolutionary process are the main factors determining the course of human events.

> No social, economic, military or ideological development takes place anywhere without being influenced by the world revolutionary process. This is the epoch of the world revolutionary process.

> Within the world revolutionary process the class struggle and the transition from capitalism to socialism is the main current. The class forces which propel the historic transition to socialism are the most stable, progressive and decisive forces of the world process.

Existing, real socialism and the advanced stage of its construction has become the central point of reference, and the standard against which all progress is measured. The building of real socialism has become the primary magnet for all forces of social progress. In the competition between world capitalism and world socialism there is a new dramatic stage. In comparing the overall quality of life, the most advanced socialist countries have caught up with and are surpassing the most advanced capitalist countries.

All developments within the world revolutionary process are adding evidence to the reality that in this epoch many class forces are involved, but it is the working class that stands at the hub. It is the working class that is determining the main content of this epoch. It is the epoch of the world revolutionary process and the transition from capitalism to socialism. (Pages 5-6, Draft MPR)

In brief, that sets the historic framework in which the struggles are taking place.

U.S. Foreign Policy

U.S. imperialism continues to maneuver and is forced to retreat in some areas. But its foreign policy line remains: that is, to mobilize the maximum forces against all sectors of the world revolutionary process, with the aim of halting or reversing that process.

There are divisions and differences within the ranks of monopoly capital. But the overall direction of the policy has not changed. U.S. imperialism pushes it to the best of its ability.

The beneficiary of this policy is U.S. finance capital and the multinational corporations which they own, and which have emerged as the "second biggest industrial power in the world next to the United States." This "stop the world" process of U.S. foreign policy is the most costly to the people of the United States.

The basic aggressive intent of U.S. foreign policy is clear. The United States is the only country with a worldwide network of military bases.

For U.S. imperialism it is not "around the world in 80 days," but in 7 hours: From Clark Air Force Base in the Philippines to its military bases in Guam; from there to its bases in Japan—to Diego Garcia in the Indian Ocean—to Australia—to two new military bases being built in the Negev Desert in Israel—and to military bases in West Germany—to England and back to the United

States—not to mention its military bases, including nuclear installations, in South Korea, Puerto Rico, Spain, Turkey, etc., etc.

And this is the country that talks about Soviet "encroachment" and the Soviet "threat." There are no signs of cutting back. Instead, there are plans and steps to increase the "U.S. military presence," especially around the oil fields.

The Pentagon brass, General Haig and Henry Kissinger testified in behalf of SALT II. But they also used the occasion to shake down the U.S. Senate for more billions in military expenditures.

After signing the new agreement with the Philippine government, specifically giving the United States the right to an "unimpeded launching of military operations from the territory of the Philippines," Secretary of State Cyrus R. Vance stated that: "Normalization of relations with China and the conclusion of this new agreement with the Philippines are closely interdependent steps to consolidating U.S. strategic positions in Asia."

The evidence is piling up that the China card is being played against the world revolutionary process. It is basically anti-national liberation, anti-socialist and anti-working class. And it is also clear that the China card is being played on cue from the Pentagon.

Africa

In Africa, U.S. foreign policy has become stuck between giving support to the fascist regime of South Africa and to the fake so-called "majority rule" in Zimbabwe, while it continues to keep a toehold in the other developing countries.

Be it Somalia, Kenya, Zaire, Egypt or Israel, U.S. imperialism in the first place is seeking military and economic benefits for itself. Preying as it does on the exploitation of other countries' natural resources, U.S. imperialism would like to create, on the African continent, a long-term reservoir of strategic and other raw materials for itself, so as to preserve its own resources in anticipation of a future "energy or some new materials crisis."

NATO's new Supreme Commander, General Rogers, openly advocates "fire brigades" of intervention, which he calls "quick reaction corps" to deal with "crisis situations."

This is a continuation of the U.S. policy of creating a reactionary "inner-African force" which was used to suppress the uprising in Zaire last Summer.

U.S. imperialism has not given up on the People's Republic of Angola. With the Maoists, it continues to support counter-revolutionary groups. And to this day it has not exchanged diplomatic recognition with the People's Republic of Angola.

The CIA, the Maoists, continue to actively support counter-revolutionary groups in Ethiopia. These are efforts to bankrupt especially the countries in Africa that have taken the path to building socialism. U.S. imperialism wants not only to protect, but to expand on the 37 percent of all its investments which are in South Africa.

The Mideast

The goals of U.S. imperialism have not changed in the Mideast either. The aim is to get oil at the cheapest possible price. It is to keep the anti-imperialist national liberation forces divided and separated from their natural ally, the socialist world. And it especially works to separate these movements from the Soviet Union. U.S. imperialism continues its efforts to reverse the Mideast sector of the world revolutionary process. They are especially focused on Iran, Afghanistan and South Yemen.

To this end, the oil monopolies, the financial institutions and the CIA work to prop up the most reactionary regimes and to manipulate Israel and Egypt as two pillars of the pro-imperialist Mideast axis.

However, this is a makeshift arrangement, founded on shifting sands. For imperialism, the shift in the balance of forces in the Mideast-Indian Ocean area has become the "arch of crisis." For the people, the "arch of crisis" is the arch of national liberation and these arches are not limited to the Persian Gulf and Indian Ocean.

Central America

The latest area to ignite is the "arch" of Central America.

After 40 years of U.S. sponsored and supported bloody dictatorships, the people of Nicaragua, with arms in hand, have said: "No more U.S. sponsored dictatorships, or colonial dictatorships of any kind." Inspired by the hero of the earlier struggles against U.S. imperialism, Augusto Sandino, the people of Nicaragua have put an end to the brutal exploitation and oppression.

We greet and hail the people of Nicaragua, the Sandinistas and the revolutionary Provisional Government of National Reconstruction.

In this struggle our international responsibility has been and is to mobilize the maximum solidarity and support to guarantee that U.S. imperialism will keep its bloody, grabbing and greedy tentacles out of Nicaragua. We will continue to do our best to fulfill this responsibility.

The victory of the forces of national liberation in Nicaragua provides many lessons. It is further proof that the forces of the world revolutionary process serve as a political and military protective umbrella. Because of it, the forces of imperialism are not free to act as they did before the world balance of forces shifted against them. This created, for U.S. imperialism, the horns of a dilemma.

In Chile, Uruguay, Paraguay, Brazil, Guatamala and other countries the forces of reaction, with U.S. imperialism, have taken a number of repressive steps in their efforts to prevent the domino effect of the victory in Nicaragua. But they will never learn. Like Somoza, they are trying to build small mud dams when the river flows at flood tide.

There continues to be differences in the ranks of monopoly capital over how to deal with the changing balance of world forces. This is a difficult problem for them because the shift is against imperialism in general, but in many ways the shift is most directly against U.S. imperialism.

Detente and SALT II

There is support for policies of detente and there is even greater support for trade and for SALT II. In fact, there is a greater popular support for SALT II than any foreign policy issue since the establishment of the United Nations after World War II.

But there is also a very vocal sector that has decided now is the time for them to make their move because the memory of Vietnam has faded and the people's resolve of "no more foreign intervention" has been forgotten. They have decided that this is the time to push for a foreign policy of confrontation and they are not without some success.

To promote their drive they have also launched a number of ultra-right coalitions, such as the National Conservative Political Action Committee, the Committee on the Present Danger, National

Right to Work Committee, the Committee for the Survival of a Free Congress and the Conservative Caucus.

These new cold war coalitions for an unlimited arms race and a foreign policy of confrontation are composed of elements of the military-industrial complex. An especially active role is played by military brass who have retired on high pensions, supplemented by corporate and secret foundation handouts, so they can continue their activities as full-time ultra-right and fascist propagandists. And General Haig, former head of NATO, has just joined them. This includes the CIA wing of the top AFL-CIO executive board, some professors with academic titles on the payroll of key universities, like Eugene Rostow at Yale, who are full-time ideologues for the ultra-right and its fascist fringe. The coalition also includes many Right-wing Social Democrats, Zionist leaders and some newspaper columnists. And last, but not least, members of the U.S. Congress.

These new cold war ultra-right gangs mainly concentrate on the legislative, electoral and propaganda arenas. They have now thrown their full weight toward a total mobilization against the ratification of SALT II.

More than worrying about caps on strategic nuclear arms, they are concerned that ratification of the SALT II treaty will put caps on their mad cold war campaign for a nuclear military confrontation.

The crucial thing about SALT II is not so much how many warheads can dance on the head of a missile, but the recognition of detente in the military arena. SALT II recognizes—for the first time since the beginning of the atomic age—the absolute necessity for military parity of the two great military powers. *This is an event of enormous historic importance. It is truly a turning point in history.* The cold war nuclear maniacs are fully aware of this. They want to stop the world before history turns the corner of military parity.

This is also the essence of the great division in the ruling class. Recognition of U.S.-Soviet parity is rejected by the ultra-right and the war hawks because it would preclude a U.S. military first-strike capability, which these lunatics actually think is possible and want to develop.

SALT II also precludes using a nuclear military threat in the effort to dictate Soviet foreign policy, to halt its aid to national liberation movements around the world.

Apart from alleviating the very real danger of an uncontrolled arms race, SALT II will also indirectly determine the shift in the balance of world forces. Measures toward arms control will free the vital economic resources in the socialist camp that can then go into the building of socialism, aid to developing socialist and newly liberated countries, as well as the national liberation movements.

There is no question about it: the defeat of SALT II could well mean the end of detente which would create a new cold war situation and the definite possibility of nuclear confrontation—by mistake, madness or design. This is precisely the reactionary purpose of the opposition to SALT II: to end detente, create a new cold war, fuel the arms race and create a nuclear first-strike capability.

This is indeed madness. But there is definitely a "Jonestown mentality" among some in Washington, which holds that the United States cannot allow the balance of forces to shift further in favor of the revolutionary currents, that the United States must, if necessary, force a nuclear showdown, and that if we are going to lose out we will take the world with us.

This is the meaning of the drive for still newer missile systems, like the MX, the Trident submarine, the Cruise missile, the Neutron bomb, etc.

The impact of the defeat of SALT II on the people and the working class—apart from the threat of a nuclear holocaust—would be tremendous.

Congressional estimates of the rise of military spending with the defeat of SALT II range from $50 to $60 billion per year.

There is a shift in the tactics of the cold warriors. As a result of the Senate hearings they evidently have concluded that SALT II will most likely be ratified. So they have shifted to their back-up position: to use whatever leverage they have for purposes of extortion—to hold up the American taxpayer for another $100 billion, to be wasted on arms build-up. And Kissinger upped the cold war ante. Besides the military extortion, he proposed to include what he calls the "geo-political" demand. The "geo-political" clause would be a demand that the Soviet Union follow the lead of the Maoists and remove itself from the world revolutionary process, turn a deaf ear to the forces of national liberation, and become pro-imperialist.

There is an old Finnish saying: Based on the 60-year record of the

Soviet Union, palm trees and tropical fruit trees will be blooming on the frozen tundra of northern Siberia before the Soviet Union even gives a thought to such concepts.

The So-called Boat People

The latest straw the forces of imperialism have grasped is the Vietnamese refugee issue. It is a situation they have largely created.

When U.S. imperialism was forced to leave Vietnam it left behind a million parasitic, declassed military personnel and hangers-on who had lived on U.S. fostered corruption. It left behind 10 million uprooted peasants who had been doused with cancer-producing Agent Orange; their rice paddies were destroyed and devastated by bomb craters and active land mines. It left behind the hundreds of thousands who had lived in U.S. barbed wire encampments without homes, a million orphans and 500,000 prostitutes. There are also close to a million Kampuchean refugees from the Pol Pot reign of terror. And there are now 4 million additional homeless Vietnamese as a result of the 1978 floods. And to this it is necessary to add the loss and sacrifice in material and human lives that it took to turn back the vicious criminal attack by the military forces of Maoism.

The Vietnamese government has been forced to take emergency measures—such as rationing and expanding the agricultural work force in order to raise food.

The Maoists, playing on feelings of Chinese nationalism, called on the Vietnamese of Chinese ancestry to "leave before it is too late." Then, to create confusion and chaos, it forcefully turned back 200,000 of these refugees into Vietnam. These are the refugees that make up most of the so-called boat people.

At the recent conference in Geneva, the Maoists and U.S. imperialism again joined forces in attacking Vietnam. Vice-President Walter Mondale, the sanctimonious, shameless degenerate in liberal garb, directed his remarks against Vietnam:

> Some tragedies defy the imagination. Some miseries so surpass the grasp of reason that language itself breaks beneath the strain—the barbed wire bondage, a floodtide of human misery.

No, Mondale was not talking about the genocidal nature of the brutal U.S. aggression against Vietnam. No, he was not making a speech at an anniversary meeting of the most inhuman bestial act of all acts in human history—the bombing of Hiroshima and Nagasaki. There is no limit to the degeneracy of capitalist politicans.

This U.S.-Maoist orchestrated attack on Vietnam will fail. The people of Vietnam are slowly, and with great difficulty, transforming their devastated land and are building a new life, a new socialist society.

Those elements in Vietnam who do not have the necessary social consciousness, who do not want to work, who are determined to live corrupt lives or to be petty entrepreneurs are free to leave. It is unfortunate that some are misled and leave because of illusions about life in the capitalist world. But their misfortune cannot be blamed on the new society, which offers them every opportunity to work, to live in a land of equality and to help build a good and prosperous life. It is tragic that these people, either because of backwardness or ignorance, have been misled into jumping from the sturdy, new ship of socialism into the rusty, slowly sinking ship of capitalism.

5

Domestic Politics

Meanwhile, on the homefront the disappointments, frustrations and mass anger are stoking the fires of broad-based fightback movements.

Related but separate coalitions are sprouting like mushrooms after a heavy rain. Just to name a few: the Progressive Alliance, headed by Douglas Fraser, President of the United Auto Workers (UAW); Citizens-Labor Energy Coalition, headed by William Winpisinger, President, International Association of Machinists (IAM); the Coalition Against Inflation in Necessities (COIN); the SOS, a coalition to fight against cuts in social security, with some 175 affiliated organizations; the Committee for Affirmative Action; the

Coalition for a New Foreign and Domestic Policy; the Congressional Black and Hispanic Caucus; the various anti-nuclear coalitions; the Coalition of Black Trade Unionists (CBTU); Trade Unionists for Action and Democracy (TUAD); the All Unions Committee for a Shorter Work Week, and the new Citizens Party, of which Barry Commoner is one of the leaders.

Some of the older coalitions are gaining new strength and vitality, such as the Southern Christian Leadership Conference (SCLC); the Coalition of Labor Union Women (CLUW); Women for Racial and Economic Equality (WREE); the U.S. Peace Council; PUSH; the National Alliance Against Racist and Political Repression (NAARPR); National Anti-Imperialist Movement in Solidarity with African Liberation (NAIMSAL); Mobilization for Survival and the National Coalition for Economic Justice (NCEJ).

These are but some of the emerging, or existing broad movements and coalitions. And many of them are duplicated on the state and city levels.

There are also a number of new trends and forces in this upsurge, including sections of the trade union movement who are taking a leading and often initiating role. This is most significant, with many ramifications for the movements. Also, more than in the past, most of these coalitions have a new understanding of the need to unify; to work for unity of labor with Black, Chicano, Puerto Rican and other oppressed peoples, women, youth, seniors, etc.

They reflect a rather high general anti-corporate consensus. While many of these movements focus on one or two issues, there is a much higher level of understanding of the tie-in between the domestic issues and the huge military budgets, between missiles and margarine.

There is a growing realization that we can not have both guns and butter. While there is a wide divergence of views on what to do in the field of electoral politics, there is a new understanding of both the need to enter the political arena and the relationship between the economic and electoral struggles.

In spite of the many weaknesses, there is a greater understanding, at a higher level than in the past, of the need to unify all forces and therefore, the need to take a stand in the struggle against racism. There is a growing awareness that without such a struggle unity is not possible.

What is also new is that most of the leading elements in these movements now recognize the need for a grass roots base.

Another positive aspect of this new upsurge is that there is a decrease in expressions of anti-communism. Communists do not have to fight to participate in these movements. In fact, we not only do not have to fight to participate, in most cases we are asked to join and help out. Therefore, if we are not today active participants in these movements and struggles, we have to honestly admit that the problem is of our own making.

It is very important for us to understand that these coalitions are the coming together of the main social and class forces of the rising anti-monopoly movement. They are key forces in the fight for political independence.

As you know, after a rainstorm mushrooms pop out of the soil overnight. But they also have a very short life span, mainly because they do not have a solid system of roots. That is also the weakness of most of these coalitions.

At this stage they are still mainly coalitions of leading forces. Most of the leading forces in the coalitions now do recognize the mushroom weakness. But some obviously fear mass participation. Because of this most of these movements are not yet mass action oriented. And others do not know how to proceed. But by and large, no one now places obstacles to such a development.

The mushrooming of these movements presents an unusual opportunity. It is an unusual challenge to the Party. It is a challenge because while the emergence of these mushrooms is a very positive development, they also bring with them the problems and weaknesses that are inherent in all broad mass movements. There are internal and external political and ideological pressures on them. They face difficult tactical questions. For example: How do you bring together those who think Kennedy is the answer with the people who are pushing for a new people's party or some other independent forms? Then there are the poisonous mushrooms, the dozen varieties of Trotskyites, Maoists and Hoxhaites who work to push movements into isolated corners.

To illustrate this overall development and derive some conclusions from it, we would program our Marxist-Leninist computer with the following: the great potential of these coalitions and movements; the weaknesses in their lack of grassroots formations;

the need to find the path that leads to overall unity; the need for a clear political direction; the need to strengthen them in the struggle against racism.

With this programming there is no question as to what the computer read-out would be. It would read: What is needed is the participation of the Communist Party on all levels, in all movements and coalitions.

Our contribution in this kind of situation can be unique. It can make the difference between these movements disappearing like mushrooms, or moving on to new heights of struggle. Therefore, we must spend less time assessing the weaknesses of these mass movements and coalitions, and spend more time doing something to overcome them through our participation. Because the problems of the economic crisis—inflation, housing, unemployment, medical care—will not disappear, the spontaneous mushrooming of mass movements will increase. We can be a political and ideological force only if we are involved, only if we are actively influencing these movements.

6

The Working Class

As Marxists we know that the class struggle is the primary essence of capitalism. It is the pivot around which everything else revolves. And because it is the primary essence of capitalism it is also the primary point of reference for our Party.

Because the working class is the pivotal force in the struggle for reforms, for social progress and in the struggle for socialism, our Party places its main emphasis and focus on the working class.

We have to keep restating this most basic of all basic concepts. Because while this is generally accepted in our Party, it is not always understood and it is not always the guide to our practice. It is accepted in our resolutions and speeches, but not always as a guide in our day to day activities. Most of us *talk* along class lines. But not all of us always *think* along class lines. The class struggle and the working class are accepted as a guide for teaching a class, but not always as a guide for our priorities, our emphasis and for the allocation of our time or for our resources.

No one in our Party is anti-working class. But anti-working class misconceptions and petty bourgeois prejudices do diminish the sense of class partisanship.

Since our last convention, many changes have taken place in the critical arena of the class struggle.

The class confrontation has greatly sharpened. The economic gap between the two great classes keeps getting wider. The rich are getting relatively and absolutely richer, and the workers are getting relatively and absolutely poorer.

It is estimated that last year a worker in manufacturing produced $32,000 in goods, and in return received $13,000, out of which $4,000 was deducted for taxes. In the first four months of this year workers lost 3.5 percent in real wages.

An interesting reversal of roles has taken place. In attempting to explain why there is an increase in foreign investment capital coming into the United States, *Business Week* said: "By the standards of today, the United States offers *cheap labor* and the all-too-rare plus of political stability." This was said, of course, before Jimmy Carter ran for the hills, came down and proceeded to fire everyone in and around the White House who did not come from Georgia. I am sure *Business Week* would not now boast of the "rare plus of political stability."

Besides the decline in real wages, job insecurity has emerged as a most serious problem for all workers. Layoffs resulting from automation, from instant plant closings, have become a nightmare for most workers. To these problems must be added the spreading plague of health and safety hazards. Working in industry in general has become a hazardous occupation.

Monopoly's Offensive

Some months ago Brother Douglas Fraser, president of the UAW, said: "I believe leaders of the business community, with few exceptions, have chosen to wage a one-sided class war in this country." The only thing we would change in that statement is that the business community has chosen to wage class war, *with no exceptions*. And, that if it continues to be a "one-sided war" for any length of time workers will go down to defeat. However, the recognition that it is a "class war" is a good starting point from which to make it into a two-sided class war. When the monopolies have "chosen to wage class war," policies of class collaboration are white flags of surrender.

In pursuing the class war, the monopolies are continuing their multifaceted offensive with the aim of destroying existing unions and of frustrating and blocking union organizing drives.

The Right-wing corporate slogan for "a union-free environment" is more than a slogan. It is a lodestar that guides the monopolies in their determination to deny workers their basic right of voluntary association in unions of their choice. We have not seen such open, brutal strikebreaking activities since the 1930s as we are experiencing today.

In most cases the government on all levels takes an open, anti-union, strikebreaking position. Anti-strike court injunctions have become almost automatic.

The corporations have become emboldened and encouraged because in a number of areas they have been able to break strikes and destroy the unions. An example is the success of J.P. Stevens, with the aid of the courts, in thwarting the efforts of the textile workers to organize for a whole generation. Another setback is the efforts of the United Steelworkers of America to organize Tenneco Corporation at Newport News, Virginia. The Newport struggle is not just another setback. It puts the spotlight on the failure of the trade union movement to mobilize all its resources to insure victory in a battle on labor's most important front.

George Meany's boast that "I have never walked on a picketline" has become the official policy of the AFL-CIO executive board.

Solidarity does not mean sitting it out while thousands of workers are engaged in a titanic struggle with an intransigent transnational conglomerate.

The sorry truth is that we have a militant rank and file, but with a leaderless trade union movement, up against the most highly organized coldblooded, inhuman, relentless ruling class in the world. The fact is no one speaks for the trade union movement. And neither George Meany, nor Lane Kirkland speaks for the whole Executive Council.

The COLA Formula

The fact is that the unions are now losing 52 percent of all elections held under the National Labor Relations Board (NLRB) regulations. And while the mass media makes a lot of noise about how the new labor-management contracts are a repudiation of Carter's 7 percent wage guidelines, the unfortunate truth is that, with minor variations, these contracts have not strayed very far from the old COLA (Cost of Living Adjustment) formula. They are well within—or at very best only slightly nudge—the outer perimeters of the wage control guidelines. They may soften the blow, but without exception they fail to halt the precipitous decline in the take-home pay of the workers.

The monopolies, on the other hand, use the hyped-up press reports to justify another round of price hikes. When he was head of the steel workers union, Phillip Murray said: "So what if steel prices rise—steelworkers don't eat steel." Because of that short-sighted and class collaborationist line some steelworkers don't eat much of anything, because as the steel corporations raised their prices, they priced themselves out of both domestic and foreign markets.

The gist of the COLA formula is an annual productivity wage increase, plus periodic adjustments for inflation. In practice, COLA can not redeem what is seems to promise—income stability. The purpose of the COLA formula is to remove wages as the central issue in collective bargaining and to substitute other issues such as pensions and supplemental unemployment benefits (SUB) that would have been better handled through legislation for all the workers.

We are not at this time opening a full discussion on the pros and cons of the COLA formula as implemented in various contracts. We are expressing a growing concern over their long-range impact on workers' take-home pay. In fact, the real wages of workers are the same in 1979 as they were 15 years ago.

We suggest the following for consideration and discussion: The COLA formula does not offset the full effects of inflation and taxes. In fact, it insures the relative impoverishment of workers. As these quantitative, relative declines accumulate they result in a qualitative change to absolute impoverishment.

The new problems creating a new crisis for workers are the simultaneous occurrence of high unemployment and inflation. And inflation cuts the living standards of every worker. For some time economists and spokesmen for monopoly capital have given up even talking about cures for both. They now talk about a trade-off, and that the workers must accept one or the other.

Barry Bosworth, formerly Carter's Director of Wage and Price Stability, says it clearly:

> Inflation can be brought to a halt if economic policies turned extremely restrictive. For every percentage point shaved from the inflation rate through such policies an additional one million people would have to be tossed out of work for two years.

What is new is that the trade-off options are becoming less available. It is not possible to have guns and butter. More guns mean less butter. Without some powerful, effective anti-monopoly measures it is not possible to have low unemployment and low inflation.

The only trade-off that is realistic is to trade off some of the corporate profits for higher wages; or the Transfer Amendment, trading off money from the military budget to job-creating meaningful projects.

One of the most serious problems facing the trade union movement is the fact that only a minority of workers are members of trade unions. And the percentage is declining. The trade union movement can not continue to have clout if it is a diminishing minority of the labor force.

When asked if he would prefer to have a large percentage of the work force unionized, George Meany responded: "Not necessarily. We have done quite well without it." George Meany has reached the point where it seems he wants to take the trade union movement into the cemetery with him.

The impending retirement of George Meany ought to be turned into a rousing celebration, a paid, national holiday of "thanksgiving."

But it should also be much more. Along with Meany, the trade union movement should retire the whole policy and practice of class collaboration, sever relations with the CIA, stop pimping for corporate executives and start fighting for workers' interests, stop begging at the doors of Democratic and Republican politicians and set up a fighting, independent, electoral structure. The trade union movement should stop looking for allies among the wealthy and start building a fighting people's front of labor, of the racially and nationally oppressed peoples, the poor on the land, the women, senior citizens and youth.

The impending retirement of Meany opens up a historic opportunity to raise in a new way the question of united trade union movement, a trade union movement that takes a definite position in the class struggle, that breaks up the demeaning, defeating class partnership. It is an opportune time for the Left and Center forces to unite and put the U.S. trade union movement back on the working class track.

It is one thing for the organized sector to be a minority in a period of union growth and increasing popular acceptance. It is quite another to be a diminishing minority when unions are losing ground, both relatively and absolutely.

As the unions lose ground, even relatively, their strength is sapped at the bargaining table and in the legislative chambers. The challenge of organizing the great majority who are unorganized is a critical question for organized as well as unorganized workers. It is a critical question for all the forces of progress.

With all its shortcomings, the Supreme Court victory in the Weber case can become an important instrument in the struggle against racism, especially in the industries. It provides a legal basis, a legal argument, for all kinds of affirmative action agreements. However, as is the case with any tool, if it remains on paper or in the tool chest it is of little practical value. Utilizing the Weber case victory within the context of future struggles for affirmative action programs in industry can become a basis for a qualitative leap in the struggle against racism. It can help remove a formidable obstacle. It can make a qualitative difference in the unification of the working class and trade union movement. There should be no labor contract negotiated, no grievance setup in trade union locals that do not include a concrete affirmative action agreement. This should become standard trade union procedure.

The Left-Center Force

Since our last convention many changes have taken place on all levels of the trade union movement.

There is movement even in the ranks of the AFL-CIO Executive Council. Many have become dissidents from class collaboration.

Many have moved to a more militant Center position. Only the old reactionary pigheaded die-hard core of the Meany-Kirkland gang remain, stuck in the corporate pigsty, and maintain their good standing in the Trilateral Commission, with the nuclear maniacs in the Committee on the Present Danger, and advocates of the policy of confrontation within the Atlantic Council. But, they are more and more isolated. They speak for less and less of the trade union movement.

However, the problem is they continue to speak in the name of the AFL-CIO. Reflecting the change in the ranks of the Executive Council of the AFL-CIO and the mood of the grass roots, increasingly there are new voices in the leadership of many of the national trade unions. This adds a new layer in the shift toward the Center. This is a most important development. Its significance is even greater because it is taking place simultaneously with the process of radicalization that continues in the grass roots.

On a different level and related to a different set of problems the same two kinds of processes in the 1930s made a qualitative change in the class struggle. In this period the shift towards the Center and the process of radicalization can bring about even greater changes.

Our present trade union policy has a history of some 12 years, and was basically outlined in the pamphlet, *Labor—Key Force*. It has gone through a process of clarification, development and some adjustments to reflect the changing scene.

Let me quote from an early document:

> In our trade union work our aim is to replace the policies of class collaboration with policies of class struggle.

> The central point of our emphasis and therefore our fundamental point of departure is to help build rank and file formations in every department, shop, industry, local union and central labor body.

When we formulated this policy it was not an abstraction or just a good idea. Its aim was to give direction to mass trends that were already in motion. Life has proven the correctness of this policy.

In today's world, to reflect today's realities, the policy means building coalitions of the Left and Center forces within the labor movement, coalitions that are capable of moving the whole labor movement away from the Right wing policies of class collaboration. Further, it means the need to develop the tactics and organizational forms that can capture the mood of the times, the power that is inherent in the spontaneous mass reactions to the corporate offensive.

Lenin described such spontaneous mass currents as the "embryonic level of class consciousness." That updates our policy.

Again, it is not a good idea per se, or an abstraction. It is consistent with the new level of mass currents. It is a policy that reflects the fact that the "embryonic" consciousness has developed further, to a higher level.

The question is: are the currents strong enough? Is the potential powerful enough, capable of moving the whole labor movement away from policies of class collaboration? We believe this is in the cards.

For some time, during the McCarthy period of repression, the Center forces were either non-existent or cowed into silence. In either case, they were not a force with much influence or power. They were dominated by the Right wing. In the last years, the Center forces have re-emerged as a power, initially on the grass roots level, and subsequently on leadership levels. It is to the credit of our Party that we foresaw this development when it was but a ripple on the scene.

Generally, what we call the Center is a force that is breaking with, and moving away from, the worst features of class collaboration. In life, nothing moves in a vacuum. This is true of the movement of the Center forces. Therefore, it is clear that while they are stimulated by objective factors, while they are reacting to issues, how fast they will move, on what issues they will move and what forms the movement will take depends largely on their relationship with Left forces. This is the basis for the concept and the need to work for unity of the Left and Center forces.

In working for Left and Center unity we are again working with and giving direction to trends that are already in motion. We are not inventing these trends.

It is also obvious that Left and Center unity cannot be established on the basis of a Left program. If the center forces were ready for such a program they would be Left forces. Therefore, it follows that Left and Center unity can be established only upon the most advanced position that the Center forces are ready to take.

In other words, this process of unification must start on the level of the most advanced position of the Center forces. The Left forces can not say: "Come, we welcome you." Instead, the attitude must be: "Let us reason together. Let's see what we can agree on."

This process can be started on such issues as the Transfer Amendment, ratification of SALT II, working for a shorter work week through such forms as the All Unions Committee for a Shorter Work Week. It can be established on the basis of shop issues, hours, wages, speedup and trade union democracy.

Those who reject the Left and Center concept, or keep saying they are "confused," are doing so because they do not believe there is a process of radicalization taking place in the ranks of workers. Or they do not accept that the Center forces are in the initial stages of that process. Not to accept or understand the significance of this radicalization of the working class is to miss or reject the main element, the cardinal essence of today's reality.

There are some areas where the Center forces are weak, and some areas where they do not yet take a Center position. These weaknesses should not be ignored. But they should not be made into roadblocks to Left and Center unity.

In the field of independent political action many of the Center forces remain advocates of the theory of the lesser evil. This holds them back within the orbit of the Democratic Party.

Many of those who have broken with the policies of George Meany do not yet follow a consistent class struggle policy. They have not yet accepted the idea that if you follow class struggle policies you have to involve the rank and file.

Many of them still follow the opportunistic, class collaborationist policies of not taking on the fight against racism, although many did take a good stand on the Weber case.

These weaknesses do *not* argue for less work in the trade union field. On the contrary, they argue for *more* support for Left and Center and Left unity. They argue for *more* support to building rank and file groups. This means more support for such organizations as TUAD and other industry-wide rank and file formations.

The Lesson of the Weber Case

As long as we have capitalism the struggle against discrimination based on racism will never be totally won. It is a continuous, ongoing struggle. How this is dealt with by the Center, by the Left and Center, and by Left formations is a most important question.

There are cases where the struggle against racism has been opportunistically compromised in the "interest of Left and Center unity." I think it is undeniable that a rank and file formation that does not take a position on the struggle against racism is going nowhere. An organization that does not take a position on the issues that divide it is going to remain divided.

There is a lesson in the unprecedented trade union support in the Weber case. More than usual, the issue was linked to the class self-interests of all workers.

There is racism. But there are also some wrong assumptions that either become the excuse or a coverup for not fighting racism. It is the assumption that racism is so deeply ingrained among white workers, so powerful a prejudice, that it is impossible to change them, or to in any way involve them in the struggle against racism. The experiences of struggles do not sustain such assumptions. Such assumptions also assume that, because of racism, white workers will not respond to appeals for class unity, for class self-interests, and will not develop a class consciousness.

We have to do more in mastering the art of fighting racism in concrete situations where the self-interests of the class and the struggle against racism are complementary and interrelated. It is necessary to reject racism and racist expressions. But that is not enough. What is called for is leadership that can win over white workers, clear up their confusion and replace racist prejudices with class consciousness and concepts of class unity.

In most departments or shops there are always one or two who are loudmouth racists, or racist provocateurs. They take advantage of the fact that white workers are either silent or laugh at racist jokes. How to take such a situation and turn it around is the challenge for all Communists and other progressive trade unionists. The key concept here is that the racism and the loudmouths are instruments of the boss who work against the interests of all workers. But you will be able to take on the loudmouths only if you are convinced, first, that silence does not necessarily mean support to a racist and, secondly, if you are convinced that class self-interests, that class consciousness, is a more viable current. If one is able to relate the struggle against racism to some concrete class issue in the department or shop the argument is always more effective. These are crucial tactical questions in the building of Left-Center unity.

It is easier to determine the line of demarcation between the Right and Center forces because the Right's position is more clearly definable. It is more difficult to define the line between the Center and the Left because they are both forces in the process of change, of movement. Also, while the concept of the Center forces is correct, this does not mean that the Center forces, under all circumstances, will be the same. Some Center forces tend to waver under pressure.

For example, the Center forces in leadership positions and the Center forces on the grassroots level will not necessarily have the same reactions. The Center forces on the grassroots level tend to take a more militant stand, especially on shop issues. The Center forces in the ranks of the racially and nationally oppressed workers tend to be even more militant.

It is also true that it is not always possible to have both Left-Center, and separate Left forms in every instance, in every situation, or even in every campaign or struggle. However, this should not become the excuse for giving up or not taking the initiative to establish such formations on both levels.

The Growth of the Left

Since our convention in Chicago [1975], possibly the most important development on the working-class grassroots level is the significant growth of a good healthy Left sector. In many of the plants in basic industry the Left is no longer a small isolated group. In many cases they are now the most active union force. They are Left but they are not narrow or sectarian. It seems obvious we need to give much greater attention to their development.

These Left forces tend to gravitate and move toward associations with those who are ready to take more advanced class positions, those who are more militant and advanced, including in the struggle against racism. They tend to move toward those who take more advanced positions on political independence and who are ready to work with Communists, even if still being influenced by anti-communism.

The concepts of Left-Center unity, and Left unity are concepts of struggle. They have meaning only within the context of struggles and specific forces. They have meaning only within the context of moving workers, leading workers in struggle. Within these formations there are some specific problems which we in the Party have to focus on.

A large component of the Left sector is composed precisely of those who see the need for militant activity. Often these groups are new in industry, and some still have many petty-bourgeois ideas, influences from their previous experiences. In many cases they are workers with little or no accumulated seniority rights. They are very often starting at the bottom. And often they are young. They include a large number of racially and nationally oppressed workers who daily must contend with humiliating attacks. These workers often proceed first from the viewpoint of moral indignation—that is, "It's not right. How can they do this to us?"

Having reached the point where they have decided to act, they often want to act NOW. They have no time to wait. This is, of course, a source of great strength for the movement, when it is directed into class channels, into tactics of mass struggle. At the same time, it has at times led to problems, since they cannot understand or refuse to accept the concept of, and the necessity for, unity. These workers have difficulty with the concept of unity because it is often necessary—in order to establish Left and Center unity—to compromise, to adjust, especially tactically, with less militant workers. The result is that often there is a revolving door of these militant elements within the rank-and-file movements. And to some extent, even in the Party.

Some of these workers fall for the demagogy of phony Left sects because they sound militant and radical. After being drawn into playing irresponsible games with militancy most of them become disillusioned not only with the Left sects, but also with the working class movement and the workers they work with.

As if following a master plan, with the full sanction by the corporations, small sects move from one industry to another. When their irresponsibility is exposed at one plant, they move to new ones. The corporations could not buy better union-busting forces. Some of these groups behave like union-busting provocateurs, including the use of lead pipes against trade unionists.

We have made headway, but we must work continuously to show the workers that these phony sects are not Communists, that our Party rejects and condemns their anti-working class activities. There are times when for demagogic reason they make reasonable proposals. We must become more adept at taking these proposals and turning them into mass struggles which will help to expose their real purpose.

It is precisely this problem that further argues for the need for special Left forms. Without Left forms there is a vacuum. It also points to the fact that Left forms should be more than committees on economic questions. In some cases it is necessary to consider whether the Left forms should be more than loose caucuses, whether they should combine the struggles around shop and union problems with forms of educational and social activities.

In other words, whether the Left forms should include organized discussions about political and ideological questions, including why Left-Center forms are necessary. Left forms should reflect their higher level of class consciousness. Left forms should be centers of a variety of Left activities. And, it seems to me, consideration should be given to specific Left actions on some issues that the Center is not ready for.

Experience shows that there is also an absolute need for industry-wide rank-and-file forms. I may be wrong, but under the present circumstance they would be Left forms. We should put an end to all speculation about this matter. Wherever such movements have been given leadership they have made important contributions. Without them the rank-and-file groups tend to float in air. There is a need for some organized body for them to relate to. Even if this is done only through a regularly-issued bulletin or newsletter, these industry-wide forms are necessary for industry-wide initiatives and coordination.

Multi-national, Multi-racial Working Class

The statement in the Draft Main Political Resolution to the effect that: "Our working class has always been multi-racial and multi-national. But the process has now reached a new level. . . . What is new is the new level of the process of unification . . . " has been the cause of some confusion in the pre-convention discussion period.

What is not clearly understood is that this description is meant to emphasize the new level of unity, of oneness of the class. These are the objective processes that are creating the basis for our working class to think and act in class terms. The emphasis is not on one or another part of the class, but the class itself. Life, class exploitation, is the molder.

Throughout our history there have been a number of factors that have held back the development of class unity and class consciousness, factors that have kept our working class divided ideologically, politically and even, physically. In past periods, the easy access to land, the Civil War and the remnants of feudalism in the South have all acted as roadblocks to working class unity.

What the Draft places in a new way is that there are a number of more recent, newer factors that have either disappeared or do not now have the same effect. The result is a more cohesive, united, single class. And these changes facilitate and speed up the process of class consciousness.

The struggles and the process of breaking down the doors of industry in the interest of racially and nationally oppressed peoples has reached a new level. While this has not put an end to policies of discrimination, it has brought great numbers of oppressed peoples into the production process and into the ranks of the working class. It is in this context that the Supreme Court decision in the Weber case can produce important results in furthering this process, especially in upgrading and promotion of those who have been held back because of race or nationality. This is a most important change affecting the working class.

It is not too many years ago that women also were generally barred from industry. Now some 45 percent of the work force are women. This again has its impact on the working class as a whole. This also has its effects on the women's movement generally, but here we are speaking about its relevance to the working class. Here again, the new development does not eliminate the policies of discrimination, but does change the framework of that struggle.

In the not too distant past industrial development in the United States had a regional character. Now, industries have filled in the empty spaces. This has also eliminated the division of the working class into regions. The GM plant in Oklahoma City employing some 3,000 workers, who just voted for the UAW as their bargaining agent, is a case in point. As a result of this development, Oklahoma will never be the same again. And the U.S. working class will never be the same.

And there are other changes: because of the unusual resources that U.S. capitalism has been able to draw on, it has with relative ease been able to divide the ranks of the working class by pitting one section against another. In the past, its ability to create a small but influential "aristocracy of labor" was one of the methods used to divide. Very often U.S. capitalism has also been able to use the workers of one craft in one industry against another, or one region against another.

However, we are now in a different situation. U.S. monopoly capital no longer has the same resources to draw on, domestically or on the world scene. It is no longer able to do some of the things it has done in the past. For example, the critical problems produced by the new economic crisis affect all sections of the working class. Take the construction field: The construction industry, which has traditionally served as one of the bases for the creation of some "labor aristocrats," is now in a crisis and the workers have been forced to take wage cuts or are unemployed. That has served to cut the source for the fattening of "labor aristocrats."

When all of this is added up, it signifies that our working class has reached a new level of oneness, a multi-racial, multi-national, male-female working class, national in scope. These developments have prepared the working class for organizing the unorganized, for a new level of affirmative action programs, a new level of class consciousness, for class political independence, and for a new working class offensive. In a sense, these objective developments are prerequisites to enable the working class to take its place at the head of the legions fighting for social progress. These are all very positive developments.

Rank and File Forms

It is possible that our concept of rank and file forms is too narrow. In most cases they are not "the meeting is called to order" kind. They are more on the order of: "Well, what do you think we ought to do?" kind. Some are Left, some are Left-Center, some are Black and white, some are Black, some are only the young and some only women.

Take the 30,000 affirmative action cases that have been filed. Most, if not all, were initiated by some rank and file group. It also seems obvious that the most successful rank and file groups are the ones in the shop or on the department floor, especially to back up the griever. As to the level of rank and file groups, the need for action, for struggle, is what propels rank and file action. So they may be on many levels, Left and Left-Center; and in the process of struggle, this may shift very fast from Left to Center and, for some, into the Communist Party. It is clear that because of the fast shifts and the processes of radicalization, it is necessary for us to be ready to reflect the changes, and when necessary to change tactics while always keeping our feet on the solid earth.

The positive developments in some sections of the trade union leadership are very important. We must continue to work with them. But we must make it absolutely clear that this does not in any way replace our emphasis on the grass roots and the need for rank and file forms. In fact, the other way around is true. There is a need for greater emphasis on normal rank and file forms.

7

Afro-American Liberation

The "Draft Resolution on the Afro-American Struggle" issued by the Central Committee was prepared as a basic policy statement which goes into the longer-range trends and assessments. For the purposes of this convention this document should be considered part of the Main Political Report.

There are Supreme Court decisions, executive orders, and periodic reports and studies by presidential commissions. Presidents, their wives, and vice-presidents appear at conventions of Afro-American organizations to make speeches about some vague, abstract progress and advances, and make even vaguer promises concerning the future struggle against racism. In spite of all the talk that "there is no special system of racism," and while there is some progress, the fact is that the basic system, the basic patterns, of racial and national oppression remain intact and in full force.

While there is some decline in racist attitudes among the people in general, there is no basic change in the racist attitudes of corporations. While there is a growing working class, Black and white unity, there is also an increase in racist activity by ultra-right and fascist groups. The K.K.K. has been emboldened to march. While more Afro-Americans are elected to public office, there is also a well-organized attack against those already holding office.

There are changes and shifts, but the basic patterns of racial and national oppression have not been broken. The proof is in the economic arena.

Because racism is an instrument of capitalist exploitation for superprofits, both its use and the struggle against it are affected by the motive forces, the overall developments, trends and perspective. While it is a serious problem for most people and for all workers, for Afro-Americans the impact and the effects of the present economic crisis start from the racist levels existing before the crisis. For unemployed Black youth, the crisis starts from the pre-crisis 60 percent jobless level, passed on from one generation to the next. Inflation cuts into the living standards of all workers. But for Afro-Americans it cuts into an existing economic gap which continues to widen.

Black family incomes have declined in relation to white family incomes, from 62 percent in the early 70s to 57 percent today. The Black unemployment rate, including those who have given up looking for work and those who hold part-time jobs because they cannot find full-time employment, is 23.1 percent, or roughly one out of every four workers. Twenty-eight percent of Black families are poor, compared to seven percent of white families. The proportion of Black families in middle or upper income brackets actually declined from 37 to 34 percent in the years 1972-1978.

One dollar per gallon for heating oil is a crisis for most working class families. But for Black families in Harlem, Chicago, Detroit and other cities it comes on top of a situation where tens of thousands have gone without heat in below zero weather in past winters.

Afro-Americans need no proof. They live with the proof every day. We have to keep updating the proof because the new deception is that racism is "something in the past," "the Blacks have made it," and "the problem is now reverse discrimination."

The peddlers of the "reverse discrimination" line do not expect people to buy the full line—and most don't. These peddlers expect their line to disarm and demobilize the people. On this, they are right. For the peddlers of racism, this is only a first step. Their longer-range goals are to reverse the historic trend—to undo the victories that have been won against racism.

Racism adds a special weight and a brutality to the national oppression of Afro-Americans. It is an ideological drug. Those addicted to it need outside help. For workers, the understanding that the drug pushers are supplied by and come from the corporate suites is a most important starting point.

Affirmative Action

Affirmative action has emerged on center stage in the struggle against racism. It raises the struggle from talk to concrete action. The Supreme Court decision in the Weber case is a significant victory for affirmative action and a tribute to the broad coalition of trade unions, Black and Hispanic organizations, and other progressive groups which fought in unity to secure a reversal of the lower court decision. The response of the trade union movement, spurred on by the rank and file and organizations like Trade Unionists for Action and Democracy and Coalition of Black Trade Unionists, has been historic. The Steel Workers Union called a conference on Weber, expecting 600 elected delegates. Over 900 showed up.

Weber marks a setback for the racist opponents of affirmative action. Under the false slogan of "reverse discrimination" they had hoped to consolidate the success they won in the Bakke case. The effect of the Weber decision is to validate the consent decrees and collective bargaining agreements for affirmative action in steel, as well as similar agreements in other industries.

However, the victory in Weber is no cause for complacency. The decision is narrow in scope. It applies only to voluntary affirmative action programs—this is, to a plan on which both the employer and the union agree, and then only if a court finds the plan to be a "reasonable" one. It does not deal with the power of the courts to order such a program as a remedy for discrimination, no matter how rampant. It has no application to situations such as in the construction industry, where both employers and unions are adamantly opposed to affirmative action.

It was to limit the decision in this way that the AFL-CIO leadership joined the anti-Weber coalition and argued in its brief that courts are powerless under Title VII to impose an affirmative action program on an unwilling employer or union. Thus, preservation of the gain that was won in Weber—let alone further advances—must still be fought for.

There will doubtless be efforts in Congress to overturn the decision by amending Title VII. These must be countered by an amendment to Title VI overturning Bakke. It will take the greatest possible unity in struggle of all anti-racist forces, particuarly in the ranks of labor, to win the upcoming fight. The Supreme Court decision in the Weber case can be used to raise the struggle for affirmative action with teeth (quotas) to a new level.

Quarter-Century After "Brown"

Concerning school desegregation, this year marks the 25th anniversary of *Brown vs. Board of Education,* holding that segregated education in the public schools violates the 14th Amendment's guarantee of equal protection under the law. The decision was historic in the sense that it took the Court more than a century to arrive at this conclusion, and sixty years to abandon the vicious fiction of "separate but equal," which it had invented as the legal coverup for racism. The anniversary of the Court's belated discovery of the meaning of "equal protection under the law" is hardly cause for celebration.

A quarter-century after *Brown,* segregated education remains the rule. The situation in Columbus, Ohio, site of one of the most recent school decisions, is typical. In 1954, when *Brown* was decided, all Columbus schools were openly and intentionally segregated. Twenty two years later, half of its 172 schools remained 90 percent Black or 90 percent white. The Court, however, did not order immediate, or even prompt, correction of the Constitutional violation it found in *Brown,* but ruled that desegregation should be accomplished "with all deliberate speed." Predictably, the entire accent has been on "deliberation."

Moreover, the Berger Court has backed off from its predecessor's commitment—if only in theory—to the principle of desegregation. It reversed the lower court order in the Detroit school case on the ground that an entire metropolitan area cannot be treated as a unit since, according to the Court, the inhabitants of the white suburbs bear no responsibility for inner-city segregation and hence should not be burdened with Black children in their schools.

These and other rulings jeopardized a number of desegregation orders issued by the lower courts after years of litigation and inspired grave fears for the future of court-ordered desegregation. These fears have been somewhat allayed by Supreme Court decisions in June, upholding the desegregation orders for Columbus and Dayton and relaxing somewhat its requirements for proof of a discriminatory purpose.

However, desegregation remains subject to the whims of a Supreme Court which has the power to delay, dilute or halt it by inventing and manipulating complex legal formulas not so blatantly racist as, but not much less deadly than, "separate but equal."

Desegregation faces an even graver threat from Congressional initiatives in the form of legislation or a Constitutional amendment prohibiting busing.

The fight for equality and quality in education remains, as it did before *Brown*, a major battleground in the war to eradicate racism and rid our country of its poison.

It should be clear that the struggle against racism has emerged even more as a key element in every area of struggle. It is a key factor in the class struggle, a key issue in the struggle for working class unity, a central issue in the struggle for democracy, for detente, for SALT II and in the struggle for socialism. It is a struggle that can be won—but it is a struggle.

8

Chicano-Mexican-American Liberation

There have also been some changes in the arena of Chicano-Mexican-American liberation, but the basic chauvinism, the basic policies of national oppression and discrimination against the Chicano-Mexican-American community continues. These patterns remain intact.

In most Chicano-Mexican-American communities the per capita income remains below the poverty level. Therefore, the present economic crisis for the majority means moving downward from the already existing poverty levels. For most of the young people the prospect for a bi-lingual, quality education remains on the drawing boards. Because of the lack of bi-lingual education in many cases the dropout rate of Chicano-Mexican-American students is 50 percent. Because of the extreme racist conditions in cities like Houston, Texas, the rate is 85 percent.

The housing construction boom has bypassed the barrios. The high unemployment rate, working in low-paying and seasonal jobs, the discrimination in housing, education, medical care and culture, and the vicious police brutality all fire the struggles and movements of Chicano-Mexican-American liberation.

Much of the chauvinism affecting the whole community is centered around the drive against people without legal documents. Every so often there are widely publicized "rounds-ups" and "dragnets," as in the days of slavery. These "round-ups" and deportations continue to be a convenient way of getting rid of excess labor when the harvest is in, without paying unemployment or social security benefits.

The people without documents are blamed for the economic ills. They are projected as an economic burden when, in fact, most of them are workers who produce and pay taxes, but who, nevertheless, in most cases are without such benefits as social security, unemployment, etc. Because they are forced to work in low-pay industries they continue to be a source of extra profits. Any solution must start from the premise that it is those extra profits that must be taken out of the exploitation of the undocumented workers.

The communities of the Chicano-Mexican-American people are basically working class. Some 50 percent of the Chicano workers are basic blue-collar workers, namely, in metal, mining, aerospace, longshore, steel, auto, and they are laborers in a variety of other industries. Some 20 percent are agricultural workers.

These workers are therefore an integral part of the multi-racial, multi-national U.S. working class. They are the key section of the working class in many industries and shops. These Chicano members of the U.S. working class have a unique role in the alliance of the working class and the Chicano-Mexican-American peoples' liberation movements and struggles.

Chicano liberation has unique features because it develops mainly in the regions that straddle the United States-Mexican border. Hence, it shares both the history and traditions of both countries. The movement works and develops with two languages. It is influenced by and shares the cultures, the class struggles and anti-imperialist sentiments of both countries.

But the exploitation and oppression are an integral part of the U.S. capitalist system of exploitation. It is this that basically determines the trends, the social and economic outlook, the relationships and class forces within the Chicano-Mexican-American liberation movement. It is a struggle for equality. It is a struggle against the policies of discrimination in industry, in the system of education and culture. It is a struggle against the policies of national oppression by U.S. corporations and by the U.S. government.

There has always been an ongoing conspiracy between the U.S. corporations and some of the ruling class circles of Mexico on how to exploit the border situation. Mainly it has been at the expense of the people and workers of Mexico. In the past it involved agriculture. Now the conspiracy includes industry and trade. This conspiracy includes low wages, tax ripoffs on both sides, and using the workers on both sides. The aim is to extract more profits, from both sides. It is a perfect haven for the multinational corporations. Only a united movement of the peoples of Mexico and the United States, especially a united movement of the trade unions on both sides, can put an end to the profit conspiracy.

The Mexican Communist Party and our Party have taken some new initiatives in this direction. It is an important question of proletarian internationalism. We must give these efforts a higher priority.

In the Chicano-Mexican-American communities there is a growing movement of independent political action. There is a growing sense of affinity and alliance with the working-class and trade union movement. There is a strong anti-corporate, anti-state sentiment. And there is a need for concrete programs of affirmative action. There is a need to create a mass democratic human rights campaign to force the U.S. government to put an end to the harassment and brutality inflicted on people without legal documents.

We must do more to mobilize a movement, especially by the U.S. trade unions, to take the super-profits out of the exploitation of undocumented workers. There is a need for a campaign to secure prevailing wage levels and for securing all the benefits and social services that, as workers, the Chicano-Mexican-American people are entitled to. This is both a human rights campaign and a struggle that will serve the self-interests of the whole U.S. working class.

In the struggle for Chicano-Mexican-American liberation we can make an important contribution by helping to find the forms and the programs that will come together in a broad Chicano-Mexican-American front that will have working relations with the trade unions and the organizations of the other racially and nationally oppressed peoples. The objective situation for such a front exists now.

9

Puerto Rican Liberation

It is one of those contradictions in life that less than 100 miles from our shores there is a thriving, independent country building socialism and another country suffering under the heel of U.S. colonial domination.

Socialist Cuba is in the midst of the most explosive building boom in its history. Without unemployment, without racism, and at an unprecedented pace, Cuba is eliminating slums and solving its housing problem. It is guaranteeing all its citizens free education, medical care, child care and old-age security. It is creating a new society which provides prosperity, security and happiness for its people from the cradle to the grave. Socialism in Cuba is but 20 years old. Twenty years ago Cuba was at the lowest level of economic and social development in the hemisphere. What a dramatic contrast!

Puerto Rico is staggering under the weight of colonial exploitation and domination—with the highest rate of inflation, with food stamps in place of wages on a large scale, rising unemployment and spreading slums. Medical care and education is now out of reach for the majority, while the U.S. corporations pile up huge profits as a result of low wages and poor working conditions. Without regard for the rights and welfare of the people or the ecology of the country, the monopoly monsters plunder and pollute the island.

The continuing bombardment of Viequez stands as a blatant example of the arrogance and inhumanity of U.S. foreign policy. It is a violation of the basic human rights of the Puerto Rican people.

U.S. imperialism has turned this beautiful island into one of the largest U.S. military bases in the world, including nuclear arms. Cuba in the Americas is a showcase for socialism, for national liberation. Puerto Rico is a showcase for capitalism, for colonial oppression.

Cuba is independent and free to build relationships with the rest of the world based on its self-interests. Puerto Rico is oppressed and tied to U.S. imperialism. The independence that Cuba has won remains the goal of the Puerto Rican independence movement.

At the moment the struggle is focused along the lines of the United Nations resolution passed last year, and on the upcoming September world solidarity conference in Mexico to which we must give our full support.

Every year tens of thousands of Puerto Rican people, impoverished by colonialism, are forced to migrate to the United States in search of a livelihood. They are oppressed and exploited from all sides.

In Puerto Rico they faced colonial oppression and exploitation. Here in the United States they face racial and national oppression, as well as class exploitation. Here they are forced to accept lower wages, inadequate housing and education, and high rates of unemployment. However, millions have also become an important component of our multi-racial, multi-national U.S. working class. They have become the key section of the class in some industries and shops, such as the garment industry of New York, or the National Steel Company plant in Lorain, Ohio.

The South Bronx in New York City is a dramatic example of the decay and dimension of the housing crisis, the hopelessness and poverty that the Puerto Rican community is forced to live in. The crisis of the cities, the crises of education, medical and child care and mass transit all have special effects and meaning in terms of the suffering and impoverishment of the Puerto Rican community.

Big Business would like to return to the past, when the people from Puerto Rico were treated as a labor pool for temporary, cheap labor, without the benefits of social services. The struggles and movements are rejecting this concept. The rising struggles are for full equality—economic and social. The working class Puerto Ricans in our country have become an important part of the U.S. working class.

There are growing movements around specific issues. There are growing movements and struggles for Puerto Rican representation in public office. They are an important element in the development of the whole movement for political independence.

The questions of Puerto Rican independence and the struggle against racial and national oppression in the United States are very closely linked. They are struggles and issues that must be of deep concern to the people of the United States as a whole, and especially to the U.S. working class. With the developments in Nicaragua, Jamaica, Grenada and other islands of the West Indies, the struggle for Puerto Rican independence is coming into sharper focus. Puerto Rico is part of the Caribbean new "arch of crisis."

The movement for independence within Puerto Rico fights under very difficult conditions. The FBI functions there as a foreign para-military police force. The Communist Party of Puerto Rico, the Socialist Party, and many others are the victims of constant harassment and provocation. The FBI uses groups as provocateurs under a left cover.

We must give greater priority to supporting and aiding the struggles that will turn the Caribbean "arch of crisis" into an arch of national liberation and socialism.

10

Native-American Liberation

A special resolution on Native-American liberation to this convention states:

> A crisis exists for Native Americans. The American Indians and Alaska Native peoples and nationalities are fighting for their very survival. They are victimized by the wanton exploitation and destruction of their lands and energy resources by powerful multi-nationals, by the U.S. Government's policy, by astronomical unemployment, extreme social and economic deprivation.

I think the resolution correctly states the essence of the question.

The growing struggles of the Native-American movements are, in the main, directed against the corporate monopolies such as Peabody Coal, Gulf and Shell Oil. Because of the special role of the state in perpetuating genocidal programs based on concepts of governmental chattel, these movements and struggles have a sharp anti-government, anti-state focus.

The extreme poverty in the slums of the reservations forces increasing numbers of Native-Americans into the new reservations of poverty in the urban centers.

The search for new sources of energy has opened a new war against Native-Americans, a new brutal campaign through legal means and plain trickery to force the people off their lands and for corporate takeover.

This new war, this new campaign of genocide, must find a new response in the ranks of the people's democratic movements. There is a crucial need for the trade union movement to take up the struggle, both as a human rights issue and because the struggle is in its own self-interests.

The struggle for Native-American liberation is a manysided and, in many ways, a complex one. One side of the struggle involves land rights and old treaties which the U.S. Government has violated and ignored. The struggles involve fishing and hunting rights. The land rights have become more critical because these lands are rich in minerals and sources of energy. The struggles are against the bureaucratic dictatorial rule on the reservations by government-appointed people who are steeped in corruption. The struggles also involve the fight against the policies of discrimination against Native-Americans who have, in increasing numbers, become a part of the U.S. working class, and face severe discrimination in the industries.

The issues are complex. But the class forces are not. The enemy is state monopoly capitalism. The struggle is against all forms of racial and national oppression. The key forces increasingly are the Native-Americans who are part of the U.S. working class.

If we are going to make an effective contribution in this struggle, we will be able to do so only if we keep in mind who the forces are, and the relationship of these struggles to the class struggle.

Unity has become the key necessity of this movement. Unity, a mass approach to struggle, and the seeking of allies are the main ingredients for victory.

11

Asian and Pacific Island Peoples

Citizens and nationals of Asian and Pacific origin are subjected to racial discrimination and chauvinist abuse. Whether it be in jobs, housing, education or any other aspect of life they are the victims of a discrimination which cuts across class lines. At the same time the large proportions of these peoples who are workers suffer class exploitation, as well as racial and national oppression.

We are champions of the economic, political, social and cultural equality of every people and support the struggles of the peoples of the different Asian and Pacific nationalities for an end to all manner of chauvinism and national humiliation.

The unfree peoples of Asia and the Pacific Islands continue the struggle for their national rights, their independence and sociopolitical progress. We stand for ending the trusteeship role assumed by the imperialist powers, the United States in the first place, and for their freedom and right to self-determination. We particularly protest the use of the Pacific Islands for U.S. nuclear testing in violation of the health and national rights of their peoples.

Our task is to support their just democratic demands and to study these questions more deeply, develop the applications of our basic policies in order to assure a working class approach, and to achieve greater mass involvement and Party building.

12

Racial and National Oppression

Racial and national oppression has been and is a built-in feature of world capitalism's drive for super-profits. It became an effective weapon especially in its operations of imperialist expansion.

Socialism marks the end not only of class exploitation but racial and national oppression and exploitation as well. It also marks the beginning of the end of racism as an ideological pattern of thought. In the capitalist world, it is very much a fact of everyday life.

There is the brutal fascist oppression of the majority of Black people in South Africa. There is the oppression of the Irish, and now the oppression of the Black immigrants in Great Britain. There is the racist discrimination and policies of genocide against Indian populations in a number of South American countries and Canada. There is the brutal oppression of the two or more million Arab peoples and the darker-skinned immigrants in Israel.

In fact, to one extent or another, racial and national oppression is a phenomenon within most of the capitalist countries. But with the exception of South Africa, Zimbabwe and a few other countries, nowhere is racial and national oppression practiced on the scale that it is in the United States.

Here in the United States racial and national oppression is an encrusted inner lining of corporate operations. Even as new nationalities arrive they are immediately classified on the ladder of national oppression, as the refugees from Vietnam are finding out. This mark will affect their employment, and their children's advancement, culture and social life.

In the United States we may not have the largest number of different nationalities. But there is no question there are more racially and nationally oppressed people here than in any other country. There are so many different nationalities that speakers and writers have difficulty determining how to deal with the total scope of the problem without always mentioning all of the racial and national groups who are victims of oppression.

I constantly receive letters listing the ones that I left out in an article or speech. I also believe many unjustly infer that the failure to mention a specific nationality or people is motivated by a lack of appreciation or sensitivity, or worse, that this omission reflects the influence of chauvinism. There are also objections to using such shortcut formulations as "and others," or "other oppressed people" or "other nationally oppressed;" and there are objections to words like "Asians," "Latinos," "minorities," etc.

I hope someone will come up with a correct scientific and shorter way of presenting the total picture of racial and national discrimination in the United States.

In addition to the Afro-Americans, Chicanos, Puerto Ricans and Native-Americans there are many other national groups and millions of others who, to one extent or another, are victims of national and racial oppression. There are the Native-Alaskans, who are now the victims of the fuel wars, the growing numbers of Spanish-speaking peoples and nationalities from the various countries of South and Central America. There are objections to the shortcut "Hispanics" also.

There are Chinese, Japanese and Hawaiian peoples, and increasing numbers of Vietnamese and Arab peoples, Filipino, Korean, East Indian and Pacific Islander peoples. There are the millions of Jewish-Americans who at this point do not sharply feel the cutting edge of economic discrimination, but anti-Semitism continues as a very active, reactionary force. And, as we know, there are some 115 different recognized Native-American-Indian peoples, nations and nationalities. And, as we also know, the total number of people who, to one extent or another, are racially and nationally oppressed in this country add up to between 40 and 50 million. But the oppression is not the same in scope or intensity.

Many of the letters I receive reflect confusion and some also show different ideological influences—racism, great power chauvinism, and petty-bourgeois nationalism. These are influences of the class enemy.

It is very important for us to have a clear understanding and appreciation of the different forces and their interrelationships. This deeper understanding is necessary in the struggle for working class unity, anti-monopoly unity, and in the struggle for democracy.

First, we should be clear that the struggle against national oppression and racism is of necessity an integral feature of every struggle. The victories and advances in the struggle for economic and social progress are inextricably tied to the struggle against national oppression and racism. Without this struggle the struggle for democracy, the class struggle, the anti-monopoly struggle, and the electoral struggles will all have a built-in limitation.

Second, we should be clear that not all nationalities are oppressed, especially those who have become integrated (with the exception, of course, of their members who have become part of the working class and are victims of class exploitation and oppression).

Third, there are different levels of oppression. Not all are of the same scope or intensity. There are differences in the level of chauvinism. Not all are discriminated against on the same level in the economic arena.

I received some letters, and even some resolutions, which refer to the question of national oppression of some specific nationality and compare it with the oppression of Afro-Americans, using phrases such as, "it is the same as," or "there is no difference." This equating and comparing does not stand the test of reality, and it is unnecessary. Giving these expressions the benefit of the best of interpretations, they reflect influences of racism.

There should be no confusion. The main root and the sharpest expression of racial and national oppression in the United States is that which is directed against Afro-Americans. All other forms and systems of racial and national oppression are related to and are fed by the racism directed against Black Americans. Any attempt to equate or to substitute this concept with another is a misrepresentation of reality and becomes a divisive concept.

Racism, white supremacy, adds a brutality, a deadly pervasive ideological poison, a scope and a depth to the oppression of Afro-Americans that cannot be compared to any other section of the oppressed nationalities. That is why the main blow in the struggle against national oppression and racism must be struck where the root is. Victories on this front will result in victories on the other fronts. When racism against Black Americans abates, the national oppression and chauvinism against all other oppressed peoples will also abate.

Our task is to find the avenues, the issues that will unite the 50 million racially and nationally oppressed peoples in alliance with the working class.

These are political concepts. We should not play numbers games. How many, by itself, is never a determining factor in political assessments. Especially, we must not use numbers either to upgrade or downgrade some other oppressed national group. This serves no purpose except to divide.

Our task is to give our very best in the struggle against racial and national oppression in every arena of struggle and to find the forms and issues that will bring the struggles together into a single stream.

We must fight against the increasing, unceasing efforts of the ruling class in this moment of crisis to divide, to set one group against another. *Unity must be our watchword.*

A correct understanding about the relationship between the struggle against racial and national oppression and the class struggle is a most important question. This is one of the very special contributions our Party makes to this struggle. This understanding rests on a correct understanding of the class struggle, the role of the working class and the forces in the struggle for national liberation. The class struggle is the controlling phenomenon of capitalist society. It determines the nature of all processes. Any attempt to bypass, to forget, to ignore this leads to floundering and going around in circles, as if in the woods without a compass.

We must reject any and all attempts to replace or equate the centrality of the class struggle and the working class with any other movement, including the method of speaking about other movements while remaining silent about the relationship to the working class. We must even reject all ideas that agree with the role of the working class in the period ahead, but do not see it now.

A proper relationship between the class struggle, the working class and the forces of national liberation provides a powerful base for the progressive movement in the United States.

13

Women's Equality

In the four years since our 21st national convention many significant changes have taken place in the movement for women's equality.

There is a greater understanding and a consciousness among all sections of the population concerning the contributions that women have made and are making in the struggles for economic and social justice, for peace and democracy. The women's movements are increasingly recognized as a necessary component of any successful struggle. This recognition has been stimulated by the rapid growth of women in the work force.

Working class women are now seen as an essential element of the struggle for women's equality. They are seen as a section without which women as a whole cannot achieve their desired equality. Consequently, the influence of working women is now a dominant trend, demonstrated by the fact that it is the issues of concern to working women which have now been adopted by the women's rights movement as a whole.

The growing influence of working women, and of Black and other nationally oppressed women among them in particular, has led to a new level of understanding and of unity among the leading women's organizations on the need to fight the divisiveness of racist ideas and patterns of discrimination.

The result has led to new initiatives more united and more persistent than ever before in the fight to win and to expand affirmative action. The concept of affirmative action is accepted among women active in the struggle for equality as crucial for all women, and has led to deeper links and greater bonds of unity between the women's movement and the movements for racial and national equality. Women played an important, initiating and unifying role in the struggle to defeat the Weber attack on affirmative action.

The fight for ratification of the Equal Rights Amendment (ERA) reflects these qualitative changes. The demands and issues of the ERA forces are no longer limited to legal, general appeals for equal status for women. The content of the demands for ratification now centers upon:

1) The need for affirmative action in the work place, and its expansion to include those material and social conditions that will enable women to further progress toward the achievement of real equality;

2) It includes the right to equal wages and to equal access to training and educational opportunities. It incorporates a growing, a more vocal section within it that opposes the Carter wage guidelines and sees these guidelines as having special drastic effects upon women workers;

3) It includes demands for child care and for affordable national health care, which incorporates the right to maternity and abortion rights and benefits, both essential issues in the struggle for equality.

The struggle to ratify ERA now includes the active consistent support of every trade union, of the Black community, of the Hispanic, Native American and other oppressed communities. The content of the struggle to ratify the ERA now contains demands and unites forces that are moving toward a more conscious anti-racist, anti-monopoly, pro-labor stance. It is clear that the struggle for the ratification of the ERA must get a much higher priority in states like Illinois, Florida, Missouri and Virginia. It must get a higher priority especially by the trade unions, by all progressive and democratic forces, and by our Party. I think our active support can make the difference.

The women's political caucus movements and the struggle to break down the electoral barriers for women candidates has emerged as a very important area of activity. By and large, the two old parties put up token candidates to snare the votes of women.

But they pull the purse strings tight when it comes to supporting women candidates. As a result, women candidates have not done well in recent elections.

The attitude of Big Business is that women should be in the surplus labor pool, or at home, and definitely not in the legislative chambers. Because of this, in electoral politics the women's movements tend to be more anti-monopoly and more politically independent. It is also true that women candidates who tend to limit their campaigning to so-called "women's issues" do not win.

In the movements against inflation, taxes, in the struggles for decent housing and quality education, women are the leading and key force in many cases.

Working Class Women

But the most important change in the past years is the role of women as part of the working class. Over 50 percent of all women are now wage workers and 41 percent of all workers are now women. The percentages of racially and nationally oppressed women working in the labor force are even higher. That is a dramatic change. This speeded-up process of proletarianization of women is making significant changes in the working class movement, in the women's movements for equality, and in the movements against racism and national oppression. *This is an historic process.* It is not a momentary development. It is the result of and related to the struggles for equality of women and to the scientific and technological revolution.

However, the entrance of women into the labor force does not put an end to policies of discrimination against women in or out of industrial plants. Big Business, as much as possible, continues in its attempts to keep women in a lower status of a reserve labor pool and is not accepting them as part of the regular labor force. They still view working women as some momentary excursion out of the kitchen to "supplement family income." On that basis they pay female employees 40 percent of what they pay male workers for the same work requiring the same experience and education. For large numbers, the gateway to industry remains a revolving door.

Women are discriminated against in job upgrading and continue to be barred from many of the skilled trades. The fact is that most of the corporations in the basic industries have an attitude of *tolerating* women on the job, only because by law they have to. And, of course, in addition to the discrimination because they are women, the Afro-American, Chicano and Puerto Rican women are also victims of the practices of racist discrimination on every level, on every job. For these women it is a continuing battle every day, every minute!

Because many male trade union leaders are influenced by male supremacist ideas, and because they also view women workers as temporary workers from a reserve labor pool, a relatively larger section of women remain unorganized. It is changing for the better, but in most cases, the trade unions take up the special problems that arise from policies of discrimination only as a result of great pressure from women workers.

The Carter cutbacks in federal funds for child care centers have created a new crisis, an additional hardship for working mothers, especially for those who are heads of households. This creates a special kind of crisis of everyday living for women workers. This must be taken up as one of the most critical issues. There can be no equality without a system of child care at reasonable cost.

Afro-American Women Workers

Over generations, the catastrophic effects of the economic and social onslaught of monopoly on the living conditions of the Black population has created special obstacles to their ability to achieve equality, or to even rise up from the status of the most oppressed. In so doing it has also placed the Black worker, and consequently Black women workers, in a special position. In their struggle to achieve equality, they force monopoly to make concessions benefiting women as a whole.

A phenomenon characteristic of the Afro-American population has been the fact that Black women have always participated in production in greater percentages than their numbers in the population. Black women have traditionally shared as breadwinners in their families, from slavery to the present, because it has always taken two wages in nationally oppressed families to sustain life.

Black women were the first women to enter heavy industrial production, and prior to that they shared equally with men in agricultural production. Their labor has ranged from unpaid to cheap labor, to domestic and often, unrecorded labor. Frequently, the fact that they are in the labor force at all has been unrecorded, because their employers have not done so. This is especially true of domestic labor. Consequently, because of their special victimization and exploitation in the work force based on class, race, nationality and sex, Black women have accumulated a certain collective experience resulting from the struggle against oppression that has been passed down from one generation to another— through tradition, culture and in the upbringing of children.

This special consciousness includes the understanding that this is a system whose society breeds racism, discrimination and injustice, and that the source is the profits made by the rich resulting from unequal wages, education and living conditions. The very nature of their living conditions and inability to overcome the barriers of discrimination over generations have served as a collective lesson whose conclusions have been adopted by the community as a whole. The American Dream has never been realizable for Black people, and certainly not for Black women.

Consequently, the unique role of Black women in the fight for women's equality has been to raise the basic economic issues of the right to equality on the job, the right to safe and healthy conditions, the right to child care, the right to quality integrated education for children, the right to health and decent housing—the right to a life that establishes equality.

At the very height of the feminist movement, when Black women were being criticized for not participating, Black women raised these issues as the key to equality for Black people, and for women in general. This concept has largely become an accepted idea.

The shift in the class status of women is clearly reflected in the women's organizations. The women's caucus movement in the basic industries is becoming an accepted feature of the trade union structure. There is a need for such caucuses wherever there are women workers. It is interesting that there are instances where men have taken the initiative to organize caucuses of women.

With serious weaknesses, the Coalition of Labor Union Women (CLUW) does have an impact and continues to function. Women for Racial and Economic Equality (WREE), a working class oriented organization, has a broad and growing following. But there are major industrial cities where there are hundreds of members who have signed up and pay dues to WREE, but where there is no

organizational structure. As a rule, this responsibility is turned over
to a woman comrade who is already overloaded with work. If
given the support it deserves and needs WREE can reach its full
potential and make a major contribution in many areas.

The lack of support for organizations like WREE raises questions
of whether this is not a reflection of more general wrong attitudes
regarding the equality of women, the lack of understanding, and
the role of working class women and the role of the working class in
general.

While not directly related to the working class movement, organizations such as the Women's International League for Peace and
Freedom (WILPF) are making very important contributions in the
struggle for peace, against racism and in the broad anti-monopoly
struggles.

Women on the Farms

Women in farming are not only a part of the overall farm
upsurge. There is emerging a movement for liberation of women
on the farm. They are victims of special policies of discrimination
directed at farm women, for example, in the areas of social security
and inheritance taxes. And in most states the work of farm women is
legally on record as of no value.

Very often women in the farming regions are the main source of
labor for the low-paying industries that move into these areas. The
women's liberation movement has moved into the various areas
where the struggle for women's equality is more specific.

In general, these movements have closer ties with the working
class and anti-monopoly struggles. It is important to take note of
these changes in the movements and struggles. Any conclusion that
the struggle has been won, or that because there are no big
demonstrations the struggle is over, would be a serious error.

It is important to take note of the changes and developments
because they are the new basis for new breakthroughs. They create
a new mass base for such movements as the struggle for free
abortions, social security, child care, health, safety and upgrading
on the job, protective legislation and the struggle for full equality in
every area of life. Becoming a part of the industrial working class is
in itself a significant step to becoming equal.

These changes greatly add to the strength of the working class and all progressive forces. There is a need for the Party not only to take note of these changes, but to take up the struggle for women's liberation in a new way, with new vigor and determination.

Male Supremacy

Male supremacy remains a major ideological obstacle to the unity of women with other sections of the population. Because affirmative action, its expansion and enforcement, would be a significant blow to the practice of male supremacy on the job, and eventually in the community and in the household, it represents the most significant link between economic equality for women which will lead to greater social and political equality.

We must intensify our efforts on every front in the struggle for equality. Concerning the struggle against the influence of male supremacy, I believe there are some tendencies to brush it under the rug—even flagrant violations. Physical violence cannot be passed off as "a family affair," or "an emotional outburst." It cannot be tolerated—not even in the slightest in the Communist Party.

The crux of the position of the Communist Party, USA is, and has always been, that full equality for women must mean full economic rights: in the first place, the right to earn a living at any job a woman wants to pursue, under safe and healthy working conditions. For women and oppressed peoples this means the right to quality, integrated education and training and upgrading on the job—if equal access to jobs is to be a reality. For women this means the attainment of effective, quality pre-school public education, so that children and youth are not cut off from the ability to secure good jobs.

The struggle for full equality for women, especially in the changed conditions of this period, must be given a higher priority by all progressive, democratic movements, as well as by our Party. The time has come, the objective conditions have matured, for a new offensive.

14

The Youth

Each generation reflects unique problems and therefore carries the distinguishing marks of its historic period. Our youth are no exception.

The present generations are molded by the unique features of the advanced stage of the general crisis of capitalism, by the change in the balance of world forces. They are the sons and daughters of the world revolutionary process. They are growing up at a time when the cheap, easy-to-get-at sources of energy are becoming depleted. They are the post-Vietnam generations. And therefore, there is a higher anti-imperialist consciousness.

Our youth are being squeezed between high unemployment and runaway inflation. They are the post-Vietnam generations. And therefore, there is a higher anti-imperialist consciousness.

Our youth are being squeezed between high unemployment and runaway inflation. They are experiencing the highest, non-cyclical unemployment rate in history. For the first time, a majority of Afro-American youth are the victims of a lifetime of racist unemployment.

Our youth are the first generations that have been born into the epoch of the explosive transition from a world of capitalism to a new world of socialism. These are the first generations that can compare the two socio-economic systems. They are more open to Marxist-Leninist and socialist ideas. The youth of today are not wedded to capitalism. Capitalism is not offering rich inducements or long-term commitments. The youth of today are not buying the usual clap-trap.

However, they are also the generations that must resist and deal with the moral, ethical and cultural decay, the hopelessness, frustrations, depression, anger, corruption, violence and complete breakdown of the fabric of our society. Millions suffer from mental fatigue—a numbness as a result of searching, searching to no avail.

More than in the past, the youth who join the ranks of the working class do so with some experience as a multi-racial, multi-national, male-female component. There is a deeper sense of unity. It is a rich soil for the growth of class consciousness, for socialist consciousness. They are the most active section of the rank and file movements.

The peace and anti-imperialist sentiments are overwhelmingly majority sentiments. The Left, ideas of socialism and class struggle, Marxism-Leninism and real socialism are becoming mass considerations for the young generation. And they do not have hangups connected with the old balance of forces when imperialism was the top dog.

From the standpoint of working class unity we often lose sight of the composition of the class in regard to age. There are approximately 20 million young workers who are in the 20-24 age range.

In the present stage of capitalism many of the options enjoyed by past generations are closed to today's young people. This is reflected in the high level of militancy and radicalization. There is a deep, angry anti-corporate mood.

Build an All-Youth Front

The objective situation has never been more primed and ready for the development of an all-youth front that will—in a broad-consensus way—be anti-corporate, anti-racist, for jobs and world peace, for an opportunity to make a decent start in life. There is no reason why initiatives for all-youth fronts cannot be taken on city and state levels. This potential is reflected in the continuing growth and influence of the Party and the Young Workers Liberation League (YWLL).

The YWLL is very much a factor in the growing youth upsurge. The League is involved in most of the areas of mass struggle. It has developed mass ties and relationships. It has good mass policies. It is strong in the struggle on ideological questions, in the struggle against anti-communism and racism.

The YWLL, both on its own and as a key force in the Youth Council of the National Council for Economic Justice (NCEJ), has been and is the most active and consistent force in the struggle for jobs. They have been an initiating force for most of the mass actions, including the actions and conferences in Washington, D.C.

The League played a leading and decisive role in the great historic Youth Festival movement, which resulted in the broadest and largest delegation to Cuba last summer, co-chaired by James Steele, National Chairman, YWLL. This included working relations with broad forces such as leaders of trade union locals, the NAACP, Urban League, United States Students Association, Mobilization for Survival, Operation PUSH, and leaders of YMCA and YWCA, as well as the Young Democrats.

The Salute to Comrade Paul Robeson was a timely and great mass cultural and political event in which the YWLL was the leading force.

We must face the truth. There are exceptions, but as a whole the Party is not involved, nor concerned about the work in this critical area. Most will speak about the high composition of youth in mass actions—as if that constitutes the youth movement—and do nothing to help build the youth movement or the YWLL.

Most leading comrades do not accept the fact that there is a youth question in industry, or that young workers face special problems. Therefore, they conclude the YWLL has no place in industrial concentration. And even further, that there is no need for any kind of special attention to young workers as a feature of our trade union activities. The fact that we are not a factor in the organization of trade union sports is proof of this.

In practice, most districts do not accept any responsibility for building the YWLL. Similarly, League work usually is not seen as a Party assignment, but something that young comrades are doing while waiting to be given "Party" assignments.

As a result, there is little in the way of review, assistance, guidance and cadre development. The multitude of pressures on club members and leaders continually takes them away from initiating ongoing concrete steps to build the League. The cadre situation is a big part of this. So is our great distance from the problems, mood and militancy of today's youth.

This generation can be won to the working class and the Party. Young people show this in a thousand different struggles. The anti-state and anti-corporate sentiment is the widest among the youth. The radicalization process, coupled with the special oppression arising from the deepening general crisis, has created a development in which broader sections of the youth can now go further along the road of struggle for progress than was true of any previous young generation. There are extraordinary possibilities and a great potential for the development of mass democratic youth unity.

The problems of young workers are growing more acute as the new economic crisis sets in. The youth question in industry shows up in the discrimination patterns in layoffs, plant shutdowns, speedup, seniority rights, upgrading, apprenticeships, job-training and of course, wages, working conditions, union democracy and representation in leadership.

For unemployed young workers there is a need for genuine affirmative action programs, especially measures that establish plantwide seniority, that require new hiring and upgrading.

Industrial concentration and the fight for the unity of our class must take into account the youth both as a component of our class and as an ally of the working class. And particularly so with the huge buildup of more or less permanently unemployed youth whom state monopoly capitalism is now rapidly moving to forcibly draft as cheap labor for "national service" and for the military.

The bourgeois think-tanks are calling for a National Service that would involve up to 2 million youth a year working in the public sectors, including construction, public service, maintenance, etc., at the minimum wage rate or less. This could wipe out many unions. Unfortunately, many union leaders support the proposal for a National Service.

Whether in the class struggle, the struggle against racism, the struggle for democracy and peace—the mobilization of the youth must be seen as a key element that requires special approaches, special forms, special cadre, special programs. In all this the YWLL is key.

Who—if not the YWLL—will take the unique initiatives that will give these youth a sense of working class and anti-monopoly direction and mass struggle? Who—among the youth themselves—will take into account that these youth are new to struggle and accordingly require special forms and approaches to involve them in struggle, raise their consciousness and effectiveness with the introduction of strategic concepts and tactical approaches based on Marxism-Leninism? Let's face it, there are many states where we would not have been on the ballot if it were not for the YWLL.

The League can and will meet the challenges of today only with the consistent help of the Party at all levels—club, district, Central

Committee and the press. This includes consistent Party attention in helping the League carry out its mass activities, especially among young workers; attention to the stabilizing, strengthening and building of the League; attention to helping build community and campus League branches; more coverage in Party press and literature and trade union support for youth demands.

Many in the Party often see the League as an intermediary form for recruiting to the Party. But this overlooks both the independent role of the League *and* the youth movement.

The point is not only that the most advanced YWLLers come to the Party, but also, and equally important, that from the ranks of the League come thousands of class conscious fighters who will be cadre for the anti-monopoly and working class movement as trade unionists, peace activists, etc. One need not be too observant, to see, that the gap in youth work, in not building the YWLL, will be the age gap in the Communist Party of tomorrow.

The YWLL cannot do the job required with its present size. The League has developed a generally sound overall policy. It is emphasizing League-building now as well as the issues of jobs, affirmative action, SALT II, the student movement and the electoral struggle. But frankly, it does not yet have the cadre in the key districts to carry it through. The Party must actively join in with the League in helping to increase its size and influence.

15

Senior Citizens

In recent years a new social movement of great importance for the anti-monopoly struggle has arisen—that of the retired generation. Its main base is that of former workers and has a large participation of women and Black people. This movement, known as the Senior Citizens movement, has arisen in response to two developments—first, the attempt of the ruling class to treat the retirees as people who have once had their say but now are to be shunted to what has aptly been called "play pens for the elderly." But the older generation refuses to accept this status, for life without active participation in struggle is no life at all. It is only a slow death.

Second, the 23 million who are 65 or over cannot permit themselves to be silenced. Their needs have never been as great as now. The elderly generation has as much or more poverty in its ranks than any other age grouping. More than 40 percent of elderly couples live on less than $500 a month, while about 70 percent of elderly single people have incomes below $350 a month. Those who, in their working years, earned least of all—Black and other specially oppressed peoples and women workers—have a lifetime of discrimination in employment now compounded as retired people.

This shameful situation threatens to become even worse. The social security system, which began with the New Deal reforms of the 1930s, and in which attainment our Party played a signally important role, is now under general attack. Multiple schemes have been hatched to tear it apart—to raise the social security eligibility age to 68 or even 70, to pit the needs of those who are disabled, and who also receive benefits from the same fund, against the elderly.

The campaign to dismantle the social security system has its headquarters in Wall Street and in the White House.

The movement of the elderly says no to any dismantling. That is why a new coalition to "Save Our Security" has come into being, including all important segments of the progressive peoples movement, and especially the labor movement. The answer to the so-called crisis in social security funding, arising out of increasing inflation and decreased income due to mass unemployment, is not to cut security benefits. Nor is it by increasing the payroll tax, the most regressive form of taxation. It is to slash military spending and fund out of general revenue. This fight is therefore not only that of those on social security, but of all workers and the labor movement. We must help guarantee that the elderly are not pitted against those on the job, nor vice versa. Only the broadest class and people's unity can win this fight.

The movement of the elderly understands the need for political struggle and for coalition with other social and class forces. It also increasingly understands the relationship between the struggle for peace, detente and disarmament to that of meeting essential human needs. This is seen in the position adopted by the largest and most important movement of seniors, the National Council of Senior Citizens. At its June convention it took a firm and united stand in favor of Salt II as a means of promoting detente and an atmosphere leading to arms reductions.

The elderly movement is here to stay. It is a movement which is bound to grow. It is an important movement, part of the general anti-monopoly movement shaping up ahead. Our Party is highly involved now but that involvement and its content must be strengthened still more.

16

The Agricultural Scene

The scientific and technological revolution has had and continues to have an explosive effect on agriculture. It has literally uprooted and scattered the old social and economic forces.

Agricultural production is now dominated by farm units that are measured in hundreds of miles, each using fertilizers and chemicals by the trainloads, insecticides by the truckloads, and machinery in planting, growing, and processing that runs in the hundreds of millions of dollars. There are irrigation systems that surpass in capacity many of the rivers.

Conglomerates and the banks have taken over. Machinery, fertilizers, chemicals, petroleum products, the marketing process and transportation are now mostly monopoly operations.

Farming has become a capital intensive operation. This process has driven out, and is still driving out, not only the small or poor farmers, but it is squeezing out mortgaged independent owners and operators of all sizes. The tractorcades to Washington, D.C. were a reflection of this new phenomenon.

Not the small family farmers or tenant farmers, but the wage laborer, the machine operator, make up the biggest single sector of the farm population today. But even here, like the plague, the automated machinery is now moving in. One year ago the tomato harvester made its appearance. Within a year or two it will replace over 80 percent of the tomato pickers, who number in the thousands.

The agricultural workers remain at the bottom of the wage scale. The majority of these workers are also racially and nationally oppressed peoples. They are Chicano, Afro-American, Filipino. Most farm laborers do not even have unemployment insurance and the other social welfare services and benefits.

Because of the growth of Big Business in agriculture most of the agricultural workers now work in as large numbers as workers in industrial plants. They have become a part of a social labor process. This experience knits them into the multi-racial, multi-national working class.

The forced exodus of poor and family farmers continues. The policy of monopoly capital, especially the banks, is to speed up this process. And the policies of the state and the Carter Administration are aimed at helping to facilitate this forced exodus.

It is one thing to understand this historic process. It is quite another to acquiesce, to stand on the sidelines and preach to the farmers about their "inevitable demise." Even quoting Engels to this effect does not make it a good policy, or a good tactic. If that was the basis for a policy we would do nothing about organizing an anti-monopoly coalition because the rise and development of monopolies was also an "inevitable" process. Marx said that 100 years ago. However, neither Marx nor Engels suggested that a working class revolutionary party should not present a program and lead a struggle against this process and its effects.

We must take a firm stand in defense of the interests of the agricultural workers, poor and family farmers, and the independent farmers who are loaded down with impossible mortgages and debts.

The facts are that the developments in agriculture are giving rise to a strong anti-monopoly mood in the countryside. This new upsurge has a very sharp anti-corporate edge. Unfortunately, there is a higher level of understanding within the farm movements of the need to join hands with the working class and unions than the other way around. This we must change.

The agricultural and related workers are an important part of the working class. The farm movements can be won as allies to the working class in the anti-monopoly struggles. They are an important contingent in the struggle for democracy. They are an important sector in the struggle against ultra-right forces.

We have to say honestly that this is not yet recognized or appreciated by the Party as a whole. Some still talk and write, even in our own press, about the "farmers" as if there are no divisions or economic differences among them. Every so often there is a phrase to the effect that the "farmers" are the cause of high prices.

Since our last convention our Party has made progress in the area of the struggles of agricultural workers and farmers. The leadership in some districts has taken this work seriously. However, we must now expand and improve our activities in this important area of work.

17

Culture and the Arts

During our pre-convention discussion period, following contributions on industrial concentration and the Party, the largest number of articles and resolutions received was in the field of culture.

One of the themes that runs through most of the material is that the Party should place a higher priority on work in the field of culture and the arts. I think the criticism is sound.

In the past, the work in this area in most cases has been too narrowly defined. It has been limited to creating leaflets or to a cultural performance at a rally. These are important contributions, but when the work is limited to them, it is wrong. Or, culture is seen as an "extra added attraction" attached to some other area of activity—such as the department of education.

Work in the field of culture and the arts has not been viewed as an important arena of mass struggles that stands on its own. The people involved in culture and the arts face unique economic problems. The struggle around ideological questions, the struggle against racism, against monopoly domination, against corruption all take place in the forms and ways peculiar to the industries related to this field.

The full scope and depth of cultural activities directly involve millions of people. It is a mass phenomenon in our country. Therefore, it must be seen as an important area of mass work. It is in the very center of all ideological and political struggles. It is an instrument of ideological and political influence on which monopoly capital spends billions of dollars.

Our country is rich in its artistic heritage—from the traditions, dances and graphic arts of the Native American peoples to the songs, crafts and other creative achievements of the slaves brought from Africa, to the pioneers, homesteaders and immigrant laborers from Europe, Asia and Latin America—all of whom became part of the United States, infusing it with a vigorous people's multi-national cultural character.

The period of intense struggles in the 1930s, during the militant movement of the workers to organize trade unions, the mass struggles of the unemployed—the period when the Scottsboro Boys, River Rouge, and Little Steel became household words—was accompanied by a dramatic upsurge in all the arts. This was not coincidental. The artists identified with the working class and portrayed their nationwide, industrywide struggles for economic security and peace.

The Communist Party was a decisive and leading participant and supporter of these movements and helped organize many cultural activities—people's theater, film and art workshops, music and choral groups. It encouraged writers and poets to develop a working class approach to literature, a proletarian literature.

Today, despite its dominance, decadent culture does not have a monopoly in the United States. Wherever there are struggles and movements, cultural forms reflecting the heroism, the class solidarity, the fighting spirit, the spontaneous ingenuity, the modest self-sacrificing attitudes, the confidence of victory of the workers and the racially and nationally oppressed peoples, begin to emerge.

There has literally been an explosion in poetry, theater, literature and graphic arts from the midst of the racially and nationally oppressed peoples. The inspiring, growing political consciousness and movements of the Black, Puerto Rican, Chicano, Native-American and Asian peoples present us with a tremendous resource for cultural organization and struggle.

The full recognition of the importance of culture is not in contradiction to the main emphasis of our Party; it is in no way contrary to the primacy of the role of the working class, the struggle against racism, the need for peace, the goal of socialism. It is an indispensable front in these struggles.

Cultural media are vehicles for the class struggle. The arts, because of their direct and powerful impact on the minds and emotions of people, and because of their potential for changing attitudes, must be enlisted in these aims. All of our efforts to achieve the goals of the Party can be strengthened if these struggles are dramatized, sung about, shown graphically.

In much of the material that has come in for pre-convention discussion there is a recurring weakness. Working class forms are mentioned but working class content of culture is not mentioned. There are suggestions to give performances for working class audiences. But there is no mention of what the working class does and can contribute to culture and the arts, and not just to cultural performers who are workers. It is the class struggle and the working class that add a new unique content to a people's culture. We must work to draw it out and to make the connection.

Cultural forces can play a major role in all areas of Party life, from enlivening and enriching club programs to implementing Political Bureau decisions. The Cultural Section of the Party must become an integrated feature of the Party's structure. Communist cultural workers have a big responsibility.

In general, there is the theoretical and political role: to analyze cultural trends in the United States; to deepen the understanding of culture among members of the Party; to support the new people's culture, the working class cultural forms that are arising as a result of struggles for economic and human rights; to provide leadership in mass organizations that are fighting for better economic conditions, housing, education and more democratic control of jobs of cultural workers in the theaters, galleries, TV studios, classrooms, etc.; to discover and help develop new talent inside and outside of the Party, and to recruit into the Party writers, artists, musicians, actors, multimedia specialists, etc.

There is a deep need for reaffirmation of our commitment to building a people's culture which reflects the multi-racial, multi-national, male-female composition of our class, a culture which engages the people's creative spirit, a popular culture that will align itself with the struggles and movements of our people.

Why not hold an annual week-end working class, people-oriented amateur extravaganza—nationwide?

And needless to say—if we are serious about our work in the field of culture and the arts, we are going to put an end to all discussion about the need for a left magazine with Communist participation, and take the steps that will get the first issue out.

18

The Intellectual and Professional Community

The scientific and technological revolution has brought with it some important changes in the lives of intellectuals and professionals. It has brought them closer to, and into the production process and the class struggle. Their creative aspirations are on a collision course with the corporate drive for maximum profits.

The crisis of capitalist ideology has a very direct effect on the intellectual community. There is no intelligent defense of capitalism or its evil deeds. In a sense there is a new intellectual who is aware and takes the working class side in the class struggle. The new intellectuals seriously question whether there is a future under capitalism. They more and more look for new ideas in the writings of Marxists. The pillars of the old ivory tower, in which many of the old intellectuals used to while away their hours, have become very wobbly.

The new intellectuals have a deeper grasp of the world around them. They are less anti-working class. The new intellectuals are influenced by the struggles against the United States agression in

Vietnam, by the struggle against racism, by the world revolutionary process. They are influenced by the process of radicalization.

The ideological struggle is much sharper in our universities and colleges than in past periods. And it is less one-sided than in years past because Marxism-Leninism has emerged as a much greater influence. In fact, some universities employ Marxist professors. And today not all the courses in Marxism and communism are anti-Marxist and anti-Communist. Intellectuals are increasingly organizing very successful classes, seminars, forums and conferences on Marxism.

We must be honest and recognize that we have not kept up with these important developments. We are not set up adequately in order to give the necessary direction and guidance in this important area. The new Central Committee must make some decisions and plans that will correct this weakness in our work. If we do not, we are missing an historic opportunity.

19

The 1980 Elections

The 1980 election campaign is already in full swing. Not only have dozens of politicians announced their candidacies for president, but some have already withdrawn from the race.

The objective developments are having a powerful impact on the political scene. The continuing energy crisis; the growth of the anti-corporate sentiment among the people; the widespread distrust and cynicism toward all government institutions; the disarray and discord in both old parties; the unprecedented low point in popular support for President Carter; the deepening voting booth alienation; the growing mood of political independence and the widespread search for meaningful alternatives; the rising mood of anger; the new initiatives in some trade union circles for independent political action—all are having their impact and molding the framework for the 1980 elections.

The President has started one of his "save Jimmy Carter" campaigns. He is on one of his "please help me" kicks. But Carter should not be too hard on himself because many of the basic problems are beyond his reach. It's getting difficult for presidents to last a full four years.

Of course the crisis problems can be sharpened by miscalculations and wrong policies. But basically they are the problems of a system in decay and decline. When a socio-economic system decays the options open to it and its representatives disintegrate ahead of the decay.

It is a commentary on our political situation that the last president had to go on nationwide TV to proclaim that he was not a crook. This president has to get his political front-men and his wife to claim that Carter's alright, that he has all his mental faculties.

I think that we can agree that it is not Carter who is insane. The problem is that when you attempt to defend and prop up an insane system it only appears as if you are crazy. At best you are crazy together with the system.

Monopoly capital's response to this political situation is a drive to get an even more direct grip on the government apparatus on all levels. Even though the open and the concealed millionaires now comprise over half of the United States Senate, and the direct representatives of big corporations fill most of the appointed executive and secretarial posts, they still want more. There are no workers in the U.S. Congress. We are not being ruled by our political or economic peers.

But Big Business wants more. For this purpose they set up the Political Action Committees (PACs). And the post-Watergate election campaign amendments gave them a legal status. There are now over a thousand PACs which dish out millions of dollars to candidates and elected officials they support.

Because of this, the appointment as head of a Congressional committee has become a real gold mine. The *Wall Street Journal* said of these PACs: "Corporate and trade association PACs have given most of their money to incumbents, simply buying access to politicians who as often as not are moderate to liberal Democrats." This widespread and vast use of corporate funds indicates the further disintegration of traditional bourgeois democracy and makes a mockery of the boasts of free elections. The elections are neither free nor cheap. The 1976 election campaign cost an admitted 212 million dollars. Like a seat on the Stock Exchange, one Senate seat went for as high as 7 million dollars. And after the elections the payoff costs continue. It is now estimated that it costs taxpayers one million dollars per year to keep a Congressman in office.

The flood of money dispersed through the local millionaire PACs was a big factor in the defeat of such liberal Democrats as Dick Clark of Iowa, Thomas J. McIntyre of New Hampshire and a number of others who supported detente and SALT II. These same sources were also a big factor in defeating a number of Black and women candidates.

In a situation where there is a small voter turnout, huge sums of money, new computerized techniques and a monopoly of the mass media, the ultra-right candidates have the edge. It is a victory by default. This combination is creating a new kind of ultra-right threat in the field of electoral politics. This becomes a serious threat especially when liberal and progressive candidates run backwards.

The two-party system remains a blind alley for the majority of the people. Most do not see any future in this alley. But they also do not as yet see their way out of it. However, more people are putting some distance between themselves and the two old parties. Political independence continues to be an ever-larger majority viewpoint. But it remains largely unorganized and scattered. It shies away from the voting booth.

The Lesser Evil Monster

The Presidential elections are still some 17 months away. But the troublesome lesser evil monster is already making its rounds. It is true the monster is somewhat emaciated because the lesser evil pickings are rather slim. The prospect of Ted Kennedy as the lesser evil rests mainly on expectations, on hope. However, a large section of people who have become disillusioned with Carter have turned to Kennedy. And this presents a very difficult situation.

These voters face a diffcult dilemma because if Kennedy decides not to run they will be left high and dry. That is a very thin reed to rest the Presidential elections on; first, because Senator Kennedy has not indicated he will fight for more meaningful alternatives and secondly, because he continues to play cat and mouse. In today's world, any candidate that does not in any way indicate a readiness to take a stand against corporate power does not meet the standard of what is a meaningful alternative. So far, Kennedy has not done so. Chappaquiddick is not the issue.

Whatever one thinks about Ted Kennedy, the fact is that he effectively serves as a lightning rod for the rising current of political independence. Some trade union leaders and others hinge their hopes for political independence on Ted Kennedy's candidacy. To wait and see, and do nothing in the meantime, is a losing game. Therefore, from whatever standpoint, whatever happens in the primaries, the best path is that of building the house of political independence. With a structure of political independence, whoever the candidates are, the people will be in a stronger position.

Political Independence

There is movement and new activities of political independence. This includes activities in most of the unions in basic industries. But some still do not see the need to move out of the Democratic Party orbit. And their early declarations of support for some Democrats only weakens their political clout.

There is a continuing growth of movement and activity within the Afro-American community. There is a network of Black elected officials. There are movements and plans for putting pressure on the two old party conventions. The formation of the Black-Hispanic Political Caucus is an important step along the path of political independence.

Increasingly there are calls for a new party coming from the ranks of those who are for political independence. And there is one initiative that has taken concrete steps in the direction of political independence. It has registered with the Federal Election Commission and is informally called the Citizens Party. It is headed by a few liberal philanthropists with a general if somewhat vague, anti-monopoly program. It has set up offices in Washington and hired a professional political staff.

One of its chief figures is Barry Commoner, the scientist and environmentalist, who is making the energy crisis a focal point and advancing the slogan of nationalizing the energy industry, in whole or in part, a slogan which we advanced three years ago.

However, there is division in the leadership of this new Citizens Party over the question of Kennedy, with some of the leaders opposing an independent candidacy if Kennedy decides to run. The Citizens Party reportedly plans to hold a platform convention in January 1980 and a nominating convention in August.

Their plans for a convention in August—after the two major parties have made their nominations—is designed to pick up, they hope, defectors from the Democratic Party if that party nominates Jimmy Carter for re-election. This may appear to be shrewd strategy, but does not overcome the central weakness of this group, its present makeup of middle class and some intellectuals, its lack of a base in labor and the Afro-American, Chicano, Puerto Rican and other nationally oppressed communities. Without such support middle class movements of individuals can also become a divisive force. Another serious weakness is the lack of a fully defined program on both domestic and foreign policy.

Thus, it can be said at this point that the picture of independent political action is a very uneven one. There is a movement of new politics, but it remains scattered.

There is mass opposition to the Administration, a powerful anti-corporate current in the country and numerous coalitions and groupings battling corporate policies. These movements may express themselves in primary fights in the old parties, particularly in the Democratic Party, and in some state and city independent candidacies.

Some of these movements may create independent political machinery to advance their program. Some may avoid the question of a national ticket and concentrate on winning a progressive bloc in Congress or state legislatures. But if they remain separate and disunited they cannot become an effective national political force on the electoral scene. This underlines the point made in our Draft Main Political Resolution:

> It is only a united independent political form which can add the new quality that will create a political magnet which will be able to draw in the forces who are still sitting on the sidelines.

The only substantial force seeking consistently to unify all these independent forces in the direction of a people's anti-monopoly party, led primarily by labor, is the Communist Party. That has been our historic position. It remains our position and policy today.

We encourage and help to build independent anti-monopoly movements in the political arena, particularly those that arise in the ranks of labor, and we press for their unity on grassroots and national levels.

We need to break down the application of our line of political independence to the level of more practical politics. We now have a good policy waiting for spontaneous events to give it life. We are especially waiting for some national initiative to give it meaning. We have a few electoral specialists. But the Party is not involved.

To our understanding that election campaigns provide a means of mass agitation and propaganda, we have to add the concept that they are also a way to acquire political power. And political power means getting the right people elected. Our electoral work must be planned with this in mind. The election victories of Vito Marcantonio, Ben Davis, Pete Cacchione and John Bernard, and later Alva Buxenbaum, were not spontaneous events.

These were victories of candidates on the Democratic Party line, the Farmer Labor Party, the American Labor Party line and the Communist Party line. These victories were the result of careful planning, the building of independent electoral coalitions and the mobilization of the Party and the masses on the basis of winning. The concept and the goal behind the victories were the attainment of political power.

Some of the candidates ran on two lines. Such victories may be necessary before a new party can become a reality. Such electoral victories means to be tuned in on the local political process and forces. The struggle for working class, trade union political representation can serve as the magnet for such forces. The struggle for Black representation, as is the case in Philadelphia, can be the path of galvanizing the popular forces that will lead to political power.

We must take our concept of a working class in alliances with the people of oppressed nationalities, women, and youth, and turn it into a concrete electoral plan for political power in states and cities.

We must take the concept of Left-Center unity and turn it into a winning campaign, especially for working class candidates.

We must take the concept of Left unity and turn it into a concrete electoral Left coalition.

Nationally, on the state and local levels, our clubs must become active forces on the electoral scene. Yes, we are interested in political electoral power. We must run serious campaigns. Running a serious campaign means professionally designed literature, drumming up speaking engagements, getting equal media time, having a prominent office, maybe billboards, buttons, etc. It means going to the shopgates, going door to door, standing on street corners with literature, planning for election day and leafletting the polls, giving people rides—all this goes with getting out the vote. We must campaign in an election like the comrades have campaigned for the Cobo Hall meeting here in Michigan.

The Communist Campaign

To help build the new politics of political independence that will lead to an anti-monopoly people's party that can effectively challenge the two old parties of monopoly capital will be a central element of our 1980 Communist Presidential campaign.

Let us be absolutely clear on this point. Our campaign does not conflict with emerging independent political movements. On the contrary, it serves to stimulate such movements. Communists in the trade unions and communities will actively help build such independent formations, united front anti-monopoly tickets. Where possible, Communists may also be candidates on such united front anti-monopoly tickets. The campaigns of Communist candidates open doors and prepare the soil for political independence, for Left-progressive candidates.

Our campaign will put forward the most advanced program of the 1980 race, a program based on the issues arising out of the class struggle and the fight against racism, for peace, democracy and basic structural change. It will indicate the path of a giant anti-monopoly coalition and the road to fundamental revolutionary change, to socialism.

Thus, our campaign must be seen as an indispensable element of the people's anti-monopoly struggle. Our struggles and our platform can make our ticket a real choice for tens of thousands who see no meaningful alternative in the candidates of the old parties.

We can roll up a powerful vote, larger than at any previous time in the 60-year history of our Party. By so doing we will not only advance our Party, but advance greatly the entire movement for a new political alignment in our country, and in addition speed the formation of a powerful anti-monopoly people's party that can successfully challenge the two old parties of monopoly capital.

To accomplish this we will have to begin early to organize to get on the ballot in at least thirty states, breaking through the maze of anti-democratic restrictions designed by Big Business to strangle independent political action. I am confident that our Party and its many supporters can accomplish this historic task.

The Party's Legal and Electoral Status

Now we have to take up a struggle against some new obstacles in the fight for our full and unequivocal ballot rights.

History teaches that every potential threat to the two-party monopoly of the electoral process has been countered by legislation making it more difficult for independent and third party candidates to appear on the ballot. This was the case following the Progressive Party candidacy of Theodore Roosevelt in 1912, the LaFollette Farmer-Labor Party candidacy of 1924, and the Henry Wallace campaign of 1948.

History is repeating itself today. Eugene McCarthy's candidacy, our getting on the ballot in 19 states and the District of Columbia, and the growing movement for independent political action has inspired many state legislatures to place further restrictions on ballot access on the pretext that "laundry list" ballots will "confuse" voters.

The loophole in the laws of a number of states including Michigan, Texas and Florida that permitted McCarthy to appear on the ballot as an independent, without the need to gather signatures, has been plugged. And legislation has been passed or is pending in a number of states to increase the number of signatures required on petitions, or to impose other new and difficult requirements. We can expect this trend to continue into 1980.

Nor has the government been lagging behind in placing obstacles in the way of independent political action. In 1976, the Supreme Court sustained a Federal Communications Commission (FCC) ruling that the Ford-Carter debates were exempt from the equal time requirement of the Communications Act under the "bona fide news" exemption. Now Congress proposes to go further. A pending bill would repeal the equal time requirement altogether and abolish the so-called fairness doctrine, thereby giving the two old parties a monopoly of the air waves.

Moreover, in the guise of preventing another Watergate, Congress has provided for the financing of presidential primary and general election campaigns from the federal treasury. The Democrats and Republicans are the sole beneficiaries.

It is significant that Justice William Rehnquist, who obviously hopes for the emergence of a party of the extreme right, dissented from the decision upholding these subsidies. He wrote:

> I find it impossible to subscribe to the Court's reasoning that because no third party has posed a credible threat to the two major parties in presidential elections since 1960, Congress may by law attempt to insure that this pattern will endure forever.

It is high time for all those concerned with the need of keeping open the avenue for independent political action, whatever their differences on other questions, to unite in a broad coalition for the defeat of measures designed to kill off breakaway political movements, even while still in the embryo stage. Such a coalition, among other things, should consider sponsoring a federal law setting reasonable uniform requirements for access to the ballot by minor party and independent candidates for federal office.

Our Party has been slow at both national and state levels to take any initiatives on democratizing the electoral process. We must quickly correct our neglect of this important work.

Our Party must not only contend with the restrictive electoral laws and practices that confront others. We come in for special treatment.

Twenty nine states have enacted laws to bar the Party and its candidates from the ballot, either in so many words or by means of "loyalty" oaths and other devices. In addition, there is federal legislation on the subject. The McCarran Act of 1950 denounced the Party because, allegedly, it does not seek its objectives "through the democratic process of the free elective system." Four years later, Congress passed the Communist Control Act designed to make the Party's use of "the free elective system" impossible by providing that "whatever rights, privileges and immunities" the Party previously enjoyed under federal and state law "are hereby terminated."

All of these laws are plainly unconstitutional under principles established by the Warren Court in the course of the Party's winning fight against the McCarran and Smith Acts. But a number of states used them to rule the Party off the ballot in 1968 and 1972.

Moreover, quite apart from the legalities, the Party's ballot status is subject to the whim of public officials who see an opportunity to make political capital out of anti-communism.

In 1976, for example, after the Maine Party had filed petitions with more than enough signatures to qualify, the Governor wrote an open letter urging the Secretary of State to reject the petitions stating:

> *All legal arguments aside,* I firmly believe the majority of the Maine people want to be on record and want the Maine people to know that Maine is not, and has no intention of becoming, a refuge and sanctuary for the Communist Party in America.

A recent attempt to cripple the Party's electoral activity has come from another quarter. Last August, the Federal Election Commission filed suit in federal court to compel our election campaign committee to keep records and make reports to it of the names of campaign contributors. We have refused to do so in reliance on a Supreme Court decision that a minority party which can show a history of harassment by government agencies or private bodies is exempt from these disclosure requirements. Certainly, if our Party cannot qualify for this harassment exemption, no other can even come close.

Predictably, the Federal Election Commission ruled the Congressional Church Committee findings, which resulted from their investigation of the FBI COINTELPRO (Counter Intelligence Program) used against Communists, trade unions, people's organizations and leading activists, to be inadequate proof of harassment and filed suit.

To prove the Party's case out of the horse's mouth, our attorney subpoenaed all the records of FBI anti-Party operations from 1936 to date. The FBI moved to quash the subpoena as "unreasonable and oppressive," stating that it involved more than 26 million pages of files at national headquarters alone, and that it would cost the government over 36 million dollars to review them. Our attorney assured the judge and the FBI that we have no interest in agitating the inflationary spiral or adding to the federal deficit and would initially settle for the files covering only the years from 1972 to date.

The FBI has now written our attorney that it has over 90,000 pages of files *dating from 1976 alone,* all of which "have been produced in the course of an ongoing investigation," and that it is therefore thinking about refusing to disclose any of them.

An FBI refusal to produce its files should at least end the Election Commission's case. For if ordinary rules of law are applicable to the Party, one government agency cannot prosecute us for a supposed violation of law when another agency refuses to disclose the evidence which will exonerate us. In any event, I can assure you that the Party will never—and I mean *never*—under any circumstances do anything to permit the names of members and contributors who wish to remain anonymous to fall into the hands of the FBI.

The struggle for full Party legality requires attention on other fronts as well. Many trade union constitutions still bar Communists from membership, eligibility for office, or both, although these provisions are unconstitutional under controlling Supreme Court decisions and invalid under the National Labor Relations Act.

Since our last convention, the ban on visas for foreign Communist visitors has been relaxed to the point where it has been possible for us to receive delegations from the fraternal parties of Mexico and Argentina. [The ban was further relaxed at this convention where thirty fraternal delegations were present. This was an important democratic victory for the working people of the United States. Ed.] But the McCarran-Walter Act still subjects non-citizen Party members to deportation and bars them from naturalization.

Preserve and Extend Democracy

We are witnessing a monstrous effort today to turn the country around from the lessons it has learned over recent years. Writers, the kind that Upton Sinclair once aptly characterized as "prostitutes of the pen," have been hired to rewrite the recent past, with the aim of making the innocent guilty and the guilty innocent. Thus the attacks on Vietnam have the objective of ending the feeling of national shame about the cruel military intervention of U.S. imperialism. And in order to prove the cold war as justified, and the despicable roles of the CIA and FBI as honorable, articles and books have been and are being written to try and prove Alger Hiss guilty and even the noble, martyred Julius Rosenberg as a Soviet spy. Even the crimes of Watergate are being pushed out of memory, with the despicable Richard Nixon invited to the White House.

There is one aspect of FBI crimes that must be brought to public attention at this time, especially as a new FBI code of conduct being presented to Congress will only assure continuation of the same wholesale violation of civil rights that has characterized FBI existence since its establishment.

As mentioned previously, for fifteen years the FBI engaged in the COINTELPRO, a program, aimed at disrupting and destroying Left and progressive organizations in general, but concentrated in particular against the Communist Party. Out of 2,370 illegal acts directed against a multiplicity of organizations, 1,388 were specifically directed against our Party.

These illegal acts included the sending of thousands of forged postcards to individuals at their place of employment, as if coming from the Communist Party, and thus leading to their intimidation or loss of their jobs.

In many instances, journalists worked as operatives for the FBI. When Henry Winston was scheduled to hold a press conference in Boston, both the TV and newspapers were advised against any coverage of the press conference.

When Gus Hall went to Cleveland to appear on a TV interview program, the FBI arranged for 100 telephone calls to be made to the station. Although the interview was taped, it was never shown.

The FBI also engaged in inciting violence and the assassination of Party leaders, but in such a way as to appear free of having a hand in it. When the Party's national headquarters, then on 26th Street in New York City, was repeatedly bombed at night, the Party demanded from the FBI that it apprehend the bombers. The New York Office of the FBI then proposed to Hoover that the Mafia be blamed for the explosion. It forged three anonymous letters, supposedly written by Party leaders, and sent them to local Mafia leaders. The letters blamed the Mafia for the bombings. One FBI agent was so disturbed by this type of incitation that he wrote to Hoover: "We must bear in mind that if the plan is successful, a gang-type murder may be the result."

The fact is that while the effort to kill Party leaders failed, more than one militant Black leader was killed in this way by inciting war between various groups. But if it failed to assassinate Party leaders, there were some incidents in the FBI's criminal activities that were successful, not in destroying our Party, for nothing can do that, but in creating some turmoil.

Under the guise of an omnibus bill to revise the United States Criminal Code the drive to restrict democracy goes on. From Nixon's day onward efforts have been made consistently by reactionaries in coalition with "liberals" to stop dissent, to render the labor movement powerless.

The S.1-S.1437 type of legislation would, among other things, prevent demonstrations and any anti-war activity, and even discussions of such protest actions. It would limit and even prohibit strikes, picketing and boycotts. It would impose more severe sentences with almost no probation or parole. There is a greater danger of such a bill passing through the present Congress, having already passed the Senate in 1978.

The many-sided struggle for legality which the Party has been compelled to wage since the moment of its birth 60 years ago continues. We conduct it not as a matter of narrow self-interest, but as an essential ingredient of the ongoing struggle to preserve and extend the democratic liberties of all.

20

The Party

Since our last Convention in Chicago in 1975 our Party has continued to grow.

The Party has consolidated its base in many of the industrial centers. Increasingly the Party has established ties and our influence has grown in the trade union movement. We are a political factor in the mass movements for peace, SALT II, in the senior citizens' movements, in the movements for economic, political and social equality, the youth and women's movements, in the struggles against racial and political repression, the tax, housing and education movements. We are an increasing factor in the struggles for medical care and in the cultural movements. The Party is a growing influence among intellectuals and professionals.

There is a growing desire on the part of leaders of mass organizations to work and consult with the Party. These are all very important developments.

The circulation of our press—the *Daily World* and *People's World*—as well as *Political Affairs,* continues to increase. The significant growth in the circulation of *Political Affairs* is an indication of the reception and growing interest in our basic ideas based on Marxism-Leninism.

The Communist vote—from New Haven to Berkeley—continues to grow. Most of our candidates get from 10 percent to 37 percent of the vote.

The Party continues to be ideologically strong and politically united. And as you can see from this convention, the Party is in high spirits.

After such a positive assessment you may ask: How can there be any weaknesses? Well, unfortunately there are. After a more careful examination and closer scrutiny we do find some. It is not so much the weaknesses as it is that we could and should do even better.

The most obvious of our deficiencies is the fact that our Party is not big enough and we are not as strong as we should be or could be. Therefore, we are not fully measuring up to the needs or the potential of the moment. We are not fully keeping up with the objective developments. And if we agree that we are not measuring up to the possibilities and not keeping up with objective developments, then we must also conclude that the weaknesses are mainly of our own making. Therefore, they are something we can correct.

In the correcting of our weaknesses it is not enough to say we will do better. We have made that resolution on many occasions. No, we must examine what the nature of our shortcomings are, what the causes are and how to correct them.

The Clubs

In a sense the bottom line test of whether the Party is measuring up is whether our clubs are measuring up to the needs and possibilities in the area of their activities.

In the process of rebuilding the Party there was a period when it was necessary to place more than usual emphasis on projection of policies, on re-establishing the positions of the Party in general.

That is still necessary. But now we have reached the point where strengthening the work of the clubs has become a key link.

Without improving the life of the clubs we simply can not measure up to the objective developments. Without improving the work of the clubs the very correct policy positions of the Party become hollow. That is one of the central—if not the central—challenges of this convention, and for all of us after the convention.

We correctly speak about a mass Party. But well functioning clubs are a prerequisite for a mass party. There is no way we can become a mass party without the clubs functioning like clubs of a mass party.

To measure up in the first place means to measure up to the mass currents, the spontaneous mass mood and the mass movements. To be with it, means to be with the rising mass upsurge. To lead mass movements, in the first place presupposes being a part of them. Spectators sitting in the bleachers have never won ballgames.

In order to measure up, it is necessary to have a correct assessment of the characteristics of the mass currents. I will not give a full assessment of the mass currents at this point because I want to discuss them in relation to the work of the clubs.

The mass movements of this moment have some very specific, and in many ways, new and unique characteristics. The most important is that in their broadest sense the mass currents, the mass sentiments, including the ones in their embryonic stage, represent majority viewpoints.

A 75-80 percent majority of our people is for SALT II. This is not yet a majority movement. But it is definitely a majority sentiment. Our task is to close the gap between the sentiment and the movements.

The anti-corporate sentiment is now definitely a majority view. This provides a new, broader base for the anti-monopoly concept.

A great majority now openly express distrust of the two old parties. Political independence is the majority sentiment. Great majorities are against spiraling inflation and the ripoff tax structure. In its broadest sense, there is a majority sentiment against racism. The great majority are for opening up trade with the socialist countries on an equal basis. The great majority reject the policies of the Carter Administration. As never before, the overwhelming sentiment is for world peace. A majority is against the huge military budgets. The U. S. Peace Council and other peace movements are beginning to work with and to tap the potential of this peace upsurge. In fact, the objective situation is ripe for the formation of a majority peace front. A majority is now convinced we can not have both guns and butter—and the people want butter.

One important public opinion poll recently concluded that a majority of Americans now believe that, "The capitalist economic system has already reached its peak in terms of its performance as a system and is now in decline." And this poll was taken before the present energy and economic crisis.

It is important to take note that these majorities are growing and moving in a very definite progressive, Left-Center direction. These majorities stretch from the embryo sentiment to those who are ready for action.

These developments have changed the political landscape of the United States. Because of these shifts in mass pattern of thought the mainstream has changed. It is no more the passive and conservative majority sector. Its political makeup has changed. The mainstream is in turbulence. It is anti-corporate. It is for SALT II. There is anger and disillusionment in this new mainstream of American life. It has strong Left-Center currents.

There is also a new Left stream. It is not the old Left or the old new Left. There is a blossoming resurgent Left with new qualities. It is much broader, with greater links to the mainstream. It is more radical in a fundamental sense. It is more militant, but in a more responsible sense. It is more tuned in to the class struggle. It is more clearly anti-monopoly and anti-imperialist. It is more clearly anti-racist. And it is rejecting the most blatant and vulgar features of big lie anti-communism.

These changes in the mainstream and the Left stream are most important shifts in the mass patterns of thought and movements. It is the new framework for our mass united front policies. These changes are also new challenges to the Party. To measure up it is clear we must take into consideration the full scope of these sentiments and movements. But to do so we must cleanse our own political cobwebs remaining from the past. We must get out of the "we are excluded," "we are rejected," "we are pushed into the corner" and "we are a small minority" syndrome. We must forget and reject the political orphan complex. We have to become better swimmers in the big pond.

Main Weakness—Sectarianism

Because of these developments, for the present period the nature of the main weakness that holds us back from measuring up can be characterized as sectarianism—a deficiency that comes in many varieties, Left and Right.

This deficiency derives from both a lack of appreciation of the level and the scope of the mass trends and a lack of understanding of the new features of the mainstream and the Left current, as well as from not understanding or fully appreciating the unique and necessary contributions we Communists can and must make to these movements. So the deficiency is both an underestimation of the mass upsurge and the Party's role in it.

When masses are not in motion, when the waves of struggle are at ebbtide, it is necessary to pursue policies and tactics that sometimes go sharply against the stream—tactics and policies of an opposition, policies that one could call sectarian, as Karl Marx once did. We have experienced such periods. This, however, is *not* one of those periods. In a period of high tide such policies and tactics turn into their very opposite. They do not lead. They tail events.

The struggle against sectarianism requires the conscious and consistent, never-ending seeking out and nurturing of allies, especially allies who are ready to work with us as Communists.

One of tne very important features of this period, as I indicated previously, is that the number of such people on the Left is growing very fast. Increasingly such people are seeking us out and expressing the desire to consult with us. These are people who will and do disagree with us on some questions. They may be ready to work with us in only one or two areas. They will have ideological flaws of many kinds. They may have had, and may still express, anti-Party concepts and slanders. But the real truth is that if we cannot work with such people, then who the hell can we work with. The fact is that if we cannot work with such people we are not going to work with anyone—except ourselves.

In mass work, the words "working with and giving leadership to" are a very important concept. If we do not practice this concept, if we do not respect the independent character of the mass movements, we can never win their respect for our leadership. Even in mass organizations in which Communists are in leading positions they cannot be viewed or characterized as "our movements." *Only the Party is ours.*

Our relationship with mass organizations and movements must be shaped by the fact that we are not out to "take over," or to dominate administratively, because it does not serve any useful purpose. Communists must be the very best of team players. The push for Communists to run for elective office, whether in a trade union or in an ad hoc committee, must come from one's co-workers. It must be earned.

Of course there are times when differences must be discussed. But we must always remember who is the main enemy. We must be careful in our judgments. We must always use the explanatory tone. We must always take into account the sum total of facts before resorting to criticism. We must continue to master the art of discussing—not debating or arguing—while working together as allies and friends.

We must put subjective and personal feelings on the back burner. They must not be permitted to become obstacles to working with people who may sometimes irritate us. We must always meet people more than halfway in order to win them, to convince people that it is possible, necessary and even enjoyable to work with us, even if we do not agree on everything. We must never assume that we are always right.

We must not follow the petty-bourgeois Maoist line of treating all who are not one hundred percent with us as being one hundred percent against us. We simply must not tolerate such attitudes.

In this context, for example, a policy of building only Left unity in a period when Center forces are in motion is sectarianism. Left unity is a very important concept. And in the context of building Left-Center unity it is a necessary concept. But a Left unity that rejects working with the Center forces is sectarian.

Experience in united front struggles shows that differences are lessened if the Party carries on independent propaganda on issues on which there are differences. Thus, Party propaganda in the form of leaflets, pamphlets and lectures is most necessary and very helpful in our united front work, especially if our materials are explanatory and convincing.

United front, wrote Lenin, is a method of mobilizing working people who either have no special or specific philosophy but who are for democracy, or people who are under the influence of reformists, revisionists or opportunists.

On the united front, Lenin said:

> The purpose and sense of the tactics of the united front consist in drawing more and more masses of the workers into the struggle against capital, even if it means making repeated offers to the leaders of the Second and Second-and-a-half Internationals. (V.I. Lenin, *Collected Works,* Vol. 42, p. 411)

At a recent Conference of Communist and Workers Parties (Moscow, 1969) the resolution stated:

> Communists should not regard everyone who is critical of the Soviet Union or the Communist Party, or who differ on one or another issue as being anti-Communist and who must be fought and rejected as far as the united front is concerned.

In this period, when the Party is pursuing a mass policy and when the members are involved in mass movements, there are of course other kinds of problems that emerge that are of a Right-opportunist nature.

When involved in mass movements there are always pressures for Communists to act and even talk like just good old plain progressives, to talk like good anti-monopoly fighters, like good democrats, like good trade unionists, like good national liberation fighters, like good old liberals.

Now there is nothing wrong with talking and acting like good trade unionists or progressives. It becomes a weakness if our activities are limited to that level. We have more to say about reforms than reformists do. For us tactics are related to strategic objectives. Our exposes are not limited to the boss or the corporation. We expose them as links in the system.

Some who work on the level of reformists continue to go to club meetings, read our press and quote the Marxist classics. But the fact is that very often the opportunism begins to corrode the ideological and political innards. Such comrades will begin to lose their class and socialist consciousness, and in time slip into a fantasy world where they think they can get along as well and even better outside the Party. This of course is opportunism and it is also liquidating the Party.

There are warning signs of this weakness. When comrades work in mass organizations and movements and never get a subscription to the *Daily World, People's World* or to *Political Affairs,* never recruit a new member—that is a warning signal that such comrades need help. They need political and ideological help. We cannot accept as natural that a comrade works in a shop, is a member of a trade union or a mass organization for 15, 20 and even 25 years and never recruits enough to start a club of the Communist Party. Some retire without ever recruiting anyone.

Such comrades were good old trade unionists, or good old democrats and democratic fighters for all those years, but they did not live and work as Communists—ideologically, politically or personally.

We must be clear that although working with mass movements may lead to problems of Right opportunism, that must never be permitted to become a conscious or unconscious excuse for not pursuing a mass policy, for not being involved in mass struggles. That would be like deciding not to plant a garden because you may have problems with opportunistic bugs and worms.

To illustrate this point: A member of my club was asked by a mass organization she works with to run on their slate for a precinct position in the local Democratic Party primaries. After a discussion the club agreed she should run because it was a unique set of circumstances; it would broaden the club's mass contacts. And she was a part of a broader independent slate. But after agreeing, the club cautioned the comrade: "You should know that if you win the election we are going to watch you like idological hawks, so that you don't become just a good old Democrat."

I have been around long enough to know that when some in the Party say that they are "confused" or that they "don't understand" some policy or tactical question, in most cases what they are really saying is: "I don't agree with the policy." In a sense, I guess, it is the same thing, because if you don't agree you do get confused.

I believe that is the case with many who say they are confused about our emphasis and concentration on industrial workers. Some of the "confusion" is rooted in not seeing the key role history has assigned to the working class.

Industrial Concentration

It is interesting that those who are confused about industrial concentration in general are even more confused about the need to focus our work on the more basic industrial workers. There should not be any confusion. This is our policy simply because there is absolutely no other choice in the matter. That is the only way the capitalist cookie crumbles. There is no other force or section of the population that can fulfill the role history has assigned to the working class. As Engels said, the working class is *forced* to fulfill the role history has assigned to it.

Those who are confused, and others who do not give such emphasis in their daily work, obviously do not agree with our assessment—at least not deeply enough.

Aristotle said: "Men acquire a particular quality by constantly acting in a particular way." I think this applies to the working class.

I think working class attitudes, working class mannerisms and traits are preferable. But of course that is my personal preference.

However, that is not the reason for our concentration policy. It rests on more fundamental premises. Steelworkers, auto workers, machinists, miners, longshoremen, electrical and rubber workers and others in a capitalist society are not only forced to "act in a particular class way," but they occupy the positions of power. And in the period ahead they will occupy positions of political power as well. No other section or group is in that slot. The capitalist production process molds workers into a class force. They tend to have less illusions about capitalism. They have no place to go but up, and can only get there through struggle and unity. As they used to say in the Navy, "that's life." It is the only class in history that cannot find solutions to its own problems without leading in the struggles for the solutions of society's problems.

Therefore, industrial concentration is not a hobby. It is not seasonal work. It will not respond to short spurts. The year-round, everyday work of the Party must be so planned and so structured from the top to bottom that it will focus on the working class. And the more basic the industry, the sharper the focus must be. It means a focus on the shops, on working class communities, on working class communities of the racially and nationally oppressed, the working class wards and precincts, and from the urban centers to the working class suburbs.

There are sections of Chicago, New York, Philadelphia, Cleveland, Los Angeles and, in fact, in all of the urban centers where industrial concentration and the struggle against the racist patterns in housing, medical care, education, in the struggle for social, economic and cultural equality, merge into a single movement—a variety of organizations, but with a single content. It is the resolution of two sets of issues with one policy of concentration.

In our work we have to take note that the perimeters of the working class in this age of technology have greatly expanded. There are new mass categories—engineers, technicians of all kinds, teachers, clerical and government workers, and many, many others. In the last years, increasingly these new sections have adopted working class methods of struggle. Tens of millions have joined unions and conduct very militant struggles. Our Party must give greater attention to these new sectors.

However, on the other hand, we must not be influenced by the Marcusean concept that the industrial workers have faded out as a force and have been "integrated" into an enlarged middle class and now are not in a position of being the leading force in the struggle for progress or for socialism. If that was the case, then our policy of industrial concentration would be out of date.

Maybe there are also some other influences that tend to cloud our focus on industrial concentration. There have always been petty-bourgeois pressures against the concept that a revolutionary working class party must work to win the support of the *majority* of the working class.

This thinking argues that it is neither possible nor necessary to win the working class majority. That was one of Mao Tse Tung's concepts.

Mao's ideas of surrounding the cities, "political power comes from the barrel of a gun," were supportive of his anti-working class concepts, which in the end led to the physical destruction of the working class section of the Communist Party of China. His advice to our Party was always: "Don't worry about winning the majority of the working class."

Comrade Will Weinstone, who continues to work, write, research and lecture, brought to my attention the fact that the same question came up at the Third Congress of the Communist International in 1921.

Umberto Terricini, the head of the delegation from the Italian Party, but speaking for two other delegations as well, proposed that the words, "necessary to win the majority of the working class" be deleted from the resolution.

Lenin, who was at the Congress, reacted very sharply:

> If these views of Comrade Terricini are shared by two other delegations, then something is wrong in the International. Then we must say: "Stop! There must be a decisive fight! Otherwise the Communist International is lost." . . . We have not only condemned the right wing elements, we have expelled them. But, if like Terricini, people turn the fight against the rightists into a sport, then we must say: "Stop! Otherwise the danger will become too grave!" (V.I. Lenin, *Collected Works*, Vol. 32, p. 471.)

That is how deeply Lenin felt about the need to have a policy of winning over a majority of the working class.

Lenin of course won and his policy was adopted. Later, Comrade Terricini, (who is still active and an outstanding world Communist figure), wrote: "Lenin smashed our arguments to smithereens."

If we did not need to win over the majority of the working class we would not need a policy of industrial concentration. For that matter, we would also not need the policy of Left-Center unity, or Left unity. The aim of these policies is to win over the majority of the working class.

Building Our Party

Everything about the present moment strongly argues for and is witness to the need to give much greater attention—concrete planned attention—to the building of our Party.

As the mass movements grow the situation becomes more complex. The anti-monopoly movement is a mixed class bag. Each group, including sections of the capitalist class, comes in with its own specific self-interests and ideas to support such interests. This makes for vacillations and pressures for accommodations. Only those with a clear class outlook and with a revolutionary socialist perspective; only those who understand both the tremendous significance of the movement, but also its mixed class character with the inevitable internal contradictions—only those who are able to solve such problems can help play the kind of role that will insure both the success of the movement and help guide its transition to higher levels of struggle. Movements that do not get the benefit of such leadership very often die on the vine.

Thus, the question of the role of the Party, the growth of the Party, including the inner-life of the Party, must be seen not in an internal, sectarian way, not as something separate from the broad movements, but must be seen as closely tied to them and in a sense within them. The Party is an historic necessity.

Our Party's historic contributions during the building of the CIO unions can serve both as a positive and a negative example. We clearly understood the historic significance of the rise of the new industrial unions in the 1930s. But to the extent that we forgot the contradictory and diverse influences within these new mass unions, we also forgot our advanced role. So we failed, to some extent, in contributing to laying a firm foundation for the next stage, for the stage when the unions were stabilized and negotiated and signed contracts, the stage when the class collaboration pressures increased.

Without question, the most serious weakness of today's mass movements is their lack of a grass roots base. What is new is that many of the leading core are not against the idea of a grass roots base. The need to strengthen our Party clubs is not unrelated to the solution of this weakness of the mass movements.

For our Party clubs this is an historic opportunity. Each club should conduct a study: which organizations have grass roots formations in their area. If they do not, the obvious question is how to build such formations. For example, if there are no grass roots formations of organizations such as the Citizen/Labor Energy Coalition and the Progressive Alliance, then the task is how to get together with the members of the local unions, whose leadership is already involved, and how to start grass roots organizations with them.

There are no obstacles to initiating grass roots forms of organizations such as the YWLL, the National Alliance Against Racist and Political Repression (NAARPR), senior citizens groups, etc. The simple truth is that there is absolutely no possible excuse for a club of the Communist Party to live and work in isolation today. In today's world it is difficult to remain isolated.

The improved functioning of the clubs of our Party, and our unique contributions to mass movements are inseparable aspects of one central task—namely, organizing and giving leadership to grass roots formations. A grass roots base is a necessity for all mass movements. Without such a base they will quickly fall victim to the plight of the soft-rooted mushroom. Party clubs not involved with the grass roots of the mass currents cannot fulfill their vanguard role. They are political mushrooms without roots.

The problems of the clubs can be resolved only in the process of working with and giving leadership to mass currents and movements.

There really are no internal organizational, political or ideological problems of the Party which are unrelated to working out the problems of leadership of mass movements. There can be no meaningful club life without it being related to real life, to struggles. The life of the Communist Party club cannot be like the life in a cloistered abbey.

A correct understanding of a Party club's relationships with mass organizations dictates the priorities for a club. This task cannot be listed as just one of the many tasks of the club. In a sense it must be the essence of everything the club does. It must be one of the themes that runs through all discussions because it is the key link.

To make a turn in the role and life of our clubs we must change the attitude and approach of our leading bodies to the work of the clubs. The clubs are not the most important feature of the Party. They *are* the Party. The leading comrades in the clubs are not there just to represent the leadership. They are in the leadership representing the clubs and the membership.

Very often leading bodies discuss, make plans and pass resolutions for something called "the Party," which as a rule does not mean the Party clubs. What "the Party" is remains a mystery. When you don't really expect decisions to be carried out you make them in the name of "the Party."

When a club is actively engaged in mass work, the overall work of the Party takes on a different meaning. Then the Party's propaganda, agitation and educational work will deal with and blend in the issues that emerge from the mass struggles. Then the advocacy of socialism takes on an immediacy of being approached as a solution, an alternative to the existing problems. Then the study of Marxism-Leninism becomes a science—not in the realm of abstract theory, but as an approach, as a guide to struggle. Then our pamphlets and leaflets will deal with and explain the relationship between the immediate issues and the overall developments.

A Party club so involved is a club with a purpose. Such involvement is the best argument for why we need a bigger party. And planned recruiting then becomes an absolute necessity, a necessity that is not an inner-necessity, but a necessity that combines the needs of the Party and the mass movements.

There are many workers who want to join our Party, but are concerned about problems of security. In many industries this is still a very real problem. If we want to build the Party we have to take this question seriously. There has to be a structural flexibility. Not every member should belong to a club. There has to also be one-to-one relationships.

Let's face it, our shop clubs in most industries are forced to function in semi-legal, or worse conditions. This is not a permanent condition, but it is the condition existing today. Evidently some of our leading cadre have difficulty accepting this reality. Some are still insisting on getting membership lists. There is absolutely no need for this. Because the corporations encourage members of some of the Left sects to flaunt their membership is no reason we should fall for this kind of obvious provocation.

Agitation, Propaganda and the Press

This is one of those periods when the majority of our people are looking for explanations, seeking answers, wondering about the direction of events. The social and class storms have erased many of the old signposts and political landmarks. The people are looking for someone to put it all together for them. They are looking for new and more basic solutions because there is a growing feeling that "for some reason the system doesn't work," that the problems are (to use Carter's phrase) "deeper, deeper."

In our agitation and propaganda material we must give answers, solutions. Agitation and propaganda that does not contain the unique characteristics and problems of the moment is form without content.

In the period since our last convention we have greatly improved our propaganda, both in content and form. There is no question that it has a more down to earth quality. We still need, however, more pamphlets and leaflets around single issues. We need more club and district leaflets.

But more than anything else we need a new understanding, a new appreciation, a new approach, a new priority, a new style of work regarding our press because it is the main instrument for reaching the people.

There was always a need for a Marxist-Leninist press. Now the possibilities are wide open for a mass circulation. Our press must become the leading popular voice of the new mainstream and the new Left sector. The *Daily World* and *People's World,* with which we have close relations, are the best papers in the country. There is no question about that. They have greatly improved. We can be very proud of them. Needless to say, the comrades who work on these papers deserve a lot of credit. They are conscientious. They are some of the hardest workers in our movement.

We have many experiences that prove that wherever workers get to read our press on a regular basis they adopt it as their paper. Let me point to a recent experience that demonstrates how workers view the *Daily World.* And there are many other experiences like it.

The *Daily World* issue of July 5 carried a story on the victory of GE workers in their contract negotiations. The Lynn, Massachusetts GE workers did not agree with the *Daily World* estimate. They thought it was too positive. When word got around the plant about our story the *Daily World* distributors were able to give out only 200 papers. This was a big cut from the usual distribution. The workers registered a protest with our paper.

The following week the *Daily World* printed an apology and a statement from rank and file workers explaining their rejection of the contract settlement and their activities in building a vote to reject the contract.

Our apology was front page, right up front. The result was that when that issue was distributed 500 copies went out on the first shift. They ran short. A rush order of 500 was called in to the *Daily World* office for the night shift distribution. Word got around and the workers really scooped up our paper at the gates. Quite clearly, workers expect the *Daily World* to be the best, to be correct, to be on their side.

Or, another example. When the UAW issued its first statement about going into negotiations for a new contract, the shop gate sales and distributions of the *Daily World* doubled and tripled within the next weeks at the auto plants. That is a great tribute to our press. These thousands of workers felt, based on their experience, that they would get the best information, the best advice about their contract negotiations, from our press. And there are similar experiences in the house-to-house sales.

We must upgrade all methods of circulation. We have a friend here from New York City. I say a friend because he has not yet joined the Party. He proves every day that he fully understands the value of our press. He sells the *Daily World* every day on the streets—winter and summer, hot or freezing. He is averaging $23 per day in sales. If we had 100 such comrades in the country the circulation of our press would go through the roof. We could make a qualitative change almost overnight.

We need to expand our system of house-to-house circulation. That can best be done by a planned program of building community roots in those apartments, complexes and streets where workers live. Such routes serve many purposes. First, it puts us into person-to-person contact with workers, gives us an opportunity to win them over to a position of class consciousness. Through such press routes we can reach such workers where the corporations cannot finger them and then harass them. The response to the newsstand campaign in New York City, where the *Daily World* is now on 1,480 newsstands, is exciting and gratifying.

The new understanding, the new priority for our press means to put an end to a routine approach. It means planning. It means daily checkup by the leadership. It means a continuous, ongoing mobilization. While it can take place simultaneously, I think world experience has shown that a mass Marxist press circulation lays the groundwork for a mass Communist Party. This new approach must start with the daily attention, checkup and followup, by the leadership of our Party.

Our papers are good. But of course they can be better. There are times when they could be more on the ball. They should have better headlines. They should be politically and ideologically stronger and more alert. They should have a more consistent class partisanship.

Surprising though it may seem the Party does not always get a fair shake. And sometimes comrades, especially comrades who are in the frontline struggle, feel our papers could reflect more of the anger and outrage.

There is some discussion on whether our press, especially the *Daily World*, should be more of an inner-organ or more of an outer-organ. Frankly, I think life is resolving that problem. Marxism-Leninism, especially in a period of upsurge, is both an inner and outer body of thought.

Our policies, our tactics, our assessments and analyses, our criticisms are also inner and outer. The *Daily World* must find ways of reflecting this new unity of the inner and the outer.

So if we are serious about building a mass party, we have to become serious about a mass circulation for our press.

We are experiencing some very exciting developments with *Political Affairs*. In a short period, circulation has doubled. The staff and editorial board are working hard to maintain a high theoretical level with a popular style and format. We do not believe theory is only for intellectuals and scholars. If we can reach the public through newsstands, bookstores, etc., we can achieve a mass circulation. Too many still view *Political Affairs* as an inner-organ for Party cadre.

21

The Ideological Struggle

Maoism

Our basic attitude toward questions related to Maoism is stated in our Party's "Open Letter to the Central Committee, Communist Party of China." You should know that we have not yet received a reply.

Our rejection of Maoism is based on all grounds. We reject it because in its basic essence it is anti-working class. We reject it because its main orientation is to obtain small favors by doing the bidding and acting as a tool of imperialism. We reject it because it is basically anti-national liberation.

Maoism works with the most reactionary forces of imperialism in every area of the world. Their anti-national liberation activities include political and ideological pro-imperialist propaganda and the joint arming, with imperialism, of reactionary anti-liberation forces.

We reject Maoism because it advocates imperialist wars as a means of attempting to halt the world revolutionary process.

We condemn Maoism because it is conducting an active war of aggression against socialist Vietnam, Laos and Kampuchea.

We reject Maoism because anti-Sovietism continues to be its main ideological and foreign policy line.

We reject Maoism as a guide to building socialism. We reject it because it is basically bourgeois nationalist and because it is in essence anti-Marxist.

Since the death of Mao Tse Tung there have been no basic policy changes in the leadership of the Communist Party of China. There are differences within the leadership, but all the main groups continue to push the anti-Marxist, anti-working class policies of Mao. The so-called "four modernizations" is basically a program of modernizing and building up its military complex.

The Class Struggle

Our Party's positions on general questions of theory and policy rest on basic foundational timbers of the class struggle, the bottom line of our times. Issues, institutions and personalities around it go through a process of change. But the essence of the class struggle, the class forces and the main class contradiction are like *Old Man River*—they just keep rolling along.

As Engels said: "There is the old illusion that it depends only upon the good will of the people to change existing relations and that the existing relations are ideas." We work on the basis that it is the *objective* processes and the forces related to the class struggle that determine the basic behavior patterns of classes.

The capitalist class behaves the way it does because of its relationship to the economic and production process. It will continue to behave as it does until a counter class force resists or stops it. Therefore, no amount of "good will," common sense or persuasion will change its basic behavior patterns. The capitalist class does not reciprocate good deeds or favors. Monopoly capital cannot be transformed or co-opted into a force for progress or for socialism. Any attempt to do so is illusory, as well as a waste of time.

The bottom line of our times is the *class struggle*. These two words are inseparable; give up the concept of struggle and you can also forget the concept of class. Any and all ideas that there can be social progress of any kind without a struggle is as impossible as the concept of reality or matter without motion.

The element of struggle is the motion in political and social affairs. Compromises in a tactical sense are necessary. But compromises, accommodation and capitulation that give up the concept of the class struggle also give up the concept of motion—motion toward progress and socialism.

We firmly believe that bourgeois nationalism is a weapon of monopoly capitalism. It is not an instrument the working class can adopt as its own. We realize a working class revolutionary party must take into account feelings of national pride and a sense of people's patriotism. But we do not accept the bourgeois concept of nationalism that is used to cover up class divisions and class exploitation. This cannot be the outlook of a working class revolutionary party. National consciousness is one thing; nationalism is quite another matter. Our national consciousness and our concept of proletarian internationalism are not contradictory. Rather, they are intertwined strands that serve the working class and the peoples of the world well, including our working class and people.

We believe tactics are necessary. But they must never be used to ignore or corrode basic positions that are rooted in the class struggle. Tactics must be supportive of the basic policy positions in the struggle. Only ideas that are deeply rooted in reality can become a material force for changing it. Therefore, Marxism-Leninism as a science must be a reflection of reality and, in the first place, the reality of the class struggle and the class forces.

Socialism

We are still being asked: What is your Party's model for the building of socialism? We do not believe it is possible to build socialism based on models. From this, however, we do not draw the conclusion that the socialist societies being built around the world are not real, or are wrong. That has been the theme of the Trotskyite sects for 60 years. They say they are for socialism. But they are against it wherever it is being built.

Each working class, each people establishes and builds the new society as a solution to the specific nature of its own particular problems. The new society will be influenced by its own history, culture, traditions and their own unique experiences. However, the main essence of real socialism is socialist, in all countries.

No one has ever insisted that socialism must be built based on models. This is an enemy slander. This distortion has always been a slander. In the building of socialism there are no exact twins or triplets. There are no carbon or xerox copies. And no one has come up with a way of cloning socialist societies.

One of the cold war arguments against SALT II is that its ratification will lull the United States to sleep. This and other cold war anti-Soviet arguments are fast losing their credibility. The majority sentiment for SALT II demonstrates that anti-Sovietism is on the decline in our country.

Anti-Sovietism is fed by the biggest of all big lies. It starts from the false premise that the Soviet Union is a military threat. It continues along the lines that every victory against imperialism is directed by the Soviet Union, that every national liberation movement is Soviet-inspired. All rebellions, all uprisings, all protests are attributed to the Soviet Union. Therefore, those who oppose SALT II place the condition that the Soviet Union would have to give aid to the forces of imperialism in their attempts to stop the world revolutionary process.

While engaged in an active and consistent drive for detente and peaceful coexistence, the Soviet Union and other socialist countries have never, and could never have undertaken to guarantee preservation of the social status quo in the world, or halt the class and national liberation struggles bred by the objective laws of historic development.

The proof that we can now break through the old barriers and limitations and become a mass party is all around us. There has never been a better, more enthusiastic response to our policies and to our ideas. We have never had greater influence.

Many factors that in the past were negative factors have now turned into their opposite. The fact that we are a revolutionary party, a party with a revolutionary outlook, is a big plus.

In the past, the fact that our Party proclaimed its stand on proletarian internationalism was a minus in the minds of the majority. Today our relationship with the world revolutionary process, our friendship with the Communists of the Soviet Union, Cuba, Angola, Chile, Nicaragua and most of the socialist countries adds to our prestige and influence.

In the past years, many were afraid to associate with us because of persecution and harassment under the Smith Act and the McCarran Act anti-Communist laws. Now, people express admiration and respect. They are proud to associate with us.

But above all else, our people are looking for our kind of solutions. When they say: "Somehow the system doesn't work," they are also ready to say: "There must be a better way."

For all these reasons and more, the moment has arrived for a mass Communist Party in our land.

I would like to conclude this Report to our 22nd National Convention with some wise counsel from Lenin:

> . . . great periods in the history of mankind . . . present such a mass of political doctrines, opinions and revolutions, that this extreme diversity and immense variety, especially in connection with the political, philosophical and other doctrines of bourgeois scholars and politicians, can be understood only by firmly holding, as to a guiding thread, to this division of society into classes, this change in the forms of class rule, and from this standpoint examining all social questions—economic, political, spiritual, religious, etc. (V.I. Lenin, "The State," *Collected Works*, Vol. 29, p. 477.)

If we heed Lenin's advice, which remains sound today; if we hold firm to the class struggle and the classes like a "guiding thread," we will find the shortest, the least painful and the most peaceful path possible to socialism in our great land.

About the Author

Gus Hall has been the General Secretary of the Communist Party since its 17th Convention in 1959. An internationally recognized authority on Marxism-Leninism, he is the author of *Imperialism Today, The Energy Rip-Off, The Crisis of US Capitalism* and scores of booklets and articles which have been widely distributed and translated into many languages.

Born on the Iron-range of Minnesota, he has been a steel worker—a founding organizer of the United Steel Workers of America, AFL-CIO and was a leader of the important Little Steel Strike in Ohio in 1937. He has also been a member of the International Woodworkers of America, the Laborers International Union of America, and the International Association of Bridge, Structural and Ornamental Ironworkers. During World War II he was in the armed forces as a sailor in the Pacific.

Joining the Communist Party in 1927, Gus Hall became an organizer for the Young Communist League and later the leader of the Communist Party in Ohio. During the years of the McCarthy fascist danger, in the 1950s, he served an 8-year term in Leavenworth Federal Prison under a Smith Act frame-up.

In 1972 and 1976 Gus Hall was the Communist Party's presidential candidate. He is also the editor of *Political Affairs*, the Party's theoretical organ.